CHRIST THE REPRESENTATIVE

CHRIST
THE REPRESENTATIVE

*An Essay in Theology after the
'Death of God'*

DOROTHEE SÖLLE

FORTRESS PRESS
PHILADELPHIA

Translated by David Lewis from the German
*Stellvertretung — Ein Kapitel Theologie nach dem 'Tode
Gottes'* (Kreuz Verlag, 1965)

Library of Congress Catalog Card No. 67-19563

To my Göttingen friends
in hope of
a reformation of
the Church

CONTENTS

7

Contents

INTRODUCTION

Towards Personal Identity

HOW CAN ONE achieve personal identity? That is the question from which this essay starts and which it seeks to relate to the other question, what does Christ mean for our human life?

Who am I? How do I find my true self? How am I to live authentically; realize my identity? It is not simply an introvert subjectivity which anxiously asks such questions. They are the questions of man in society: a society which claims and shapes him, damages and distorts him. Nonplussed by the setbacks to rationality in this century, by the disturbing decline into self-imposed tutelage; dismayed by novel and proliferating versions of the denial of the very possibility of identity; tormented by the neuroses which civilization exacts and which mark its failure to honour its promises of humanization—man looks for a world in which it might be easier to achieve personal identity.

But every vision of a more congenial world has to be measured against the greatest of them all, the vision of the kingdom of God. Where is this kingdom and when does it appear? An inevitable question for anyone who finds it impossible simply to disregard his own experience of non-identity, who knows that it is not the individual who lives his own life but his life which is being lived for him, and that the individual has simply to submit to this 'being lived'. Yet the quiet voice of the One who died as the champion of that kingdom continues to dissuade us from any kind of scepticism, however wellfounded. Many, it is true, regard the kingdom of God and the 'secure happiness'[1] of

[1] J. S. Bach, *Christmas Oratorio*, Part III.

9

all men in that kingdom as a dream which has had its day, as mere wishful thinking. An age inimical to ideology classes it as one among many such ideologies. It makes little difference whether the kingdom is dismissed by the atheist as non-existent, whether it is sited by the Christian right outside our world altogether as something future and heavenly, or treated by the Marxist-Leninist as a kingdom which man can plan and construct. Those who have abandoned hope along with the ideologies can only smile ruefully at the vision of this kingdom. Yet the persistent voice of its champion continues to disturb even those among the hopeless who no longer notice their loss of hope.

Theology informs us that only the man who has learnt who Christ is knows and can say who he himself is. This assertion, summing up the theme of our essay, is tendentious of course, biased in favour of the kingdom in which personal identity is said to be possible. No further demonstration of man's longing for identity is offered here. It is regarded as axiomatic. Whether there ever have been or ever will be human lives not engaged in this search for personal identity cannot be demonstrated empirically or historically. Nor does this lessen the gravity of the question for ourselves. Again, while we cannot demonstrate that it is the experience of Christ which enables us to achieve identity, we can certainly reflect upon this claim. Theology will then be a reflective description of certain experiences.

Such experiences in the course of the search for personal identity can only be had within the continually changing historical conditions which prevail at any given time. Otherwise they would amount to no more than laboured efforts to prolong previous experiences in whose atmosphere man lived for a time. The historical condition under which the absolute appears today is described in our subtitle as the 'death of God', an event which has taken place within the last two centuries of European history and which conditions every aspect of life. Being a concrete event in history, it cannot be removed out of reach of fate and action, guilt and chance, refusal and renunciation. That is why the term 'atheism' seems inappropriate to describe this event. Those who commented on it while it was happening—Hegel, Jean Paul,[1] and Nietzsche, to name only a few—did not use the term; and those who regarded themselves as atheists thought it unnecessary to comment specially on the event because for them the non-existence of a supreme being was not so much an experience as an obvious fact of life simply to be observed and noted down. This distinction between atheism and the experience of the death of God cannot of course be established simply by reference to the use of words, though linguistic usage does provide a pointer.

Formally, the statement that God is dead is no different from the statement that a friend or acquaintance is dead. Whatever response such a statement may evoke, it refers to someone else's death, not one's own. But someone else's death is always a death which *affects* another person or persons, never death in the abstract. A mother's death affects her children. She is dead for *them*. Only a medical death certificate can dispense with this reference to others. *For whom*, then, is God dead? The factor determining the reference in the case of the dead is mourning, grief, shame, remembrance. The factor which determines whether men argue (within the realm of objective material nature) the merits of theism or atheism, or speak (within the realm of human history) of the death of God, is the capacity of those involved to suffer. God is not dead for these who can apply to him the statement, 'he does not exist', any more than he is alive for those who assume that 'he does exist'. Both alike are strangers to (possibly have not understood or have even suppressed) the new experience of God which characterizes our contemporary situation, the experience of the individual who finds himself insecure and alone in a completely changed world and society.

But an increasing number of people are so gripped by this experience that they can no longer reconcile it either with theism or atheism because these two positions alike betray a

[1] Jean Paul Friedrich Richter, 1763-1825.

naive, undisturbed ideological confidence. No attempt to relate
the new experience to such settled positions does justice to the
reality of the mind's oscillation between them, to its inability
either to answer or to drop the question concerning the meaning
of existence and the purpose and goal of history. This uncertainty first emerged in the nineteenth century as a prophetic
intuition, but today it has become increasingly widespread as a
fact of experience either stoically endured or consciously re-
sisted. It makes impossible the acceptance of truth as something
objective and traditional, or the hope of its attainment by a
vigorous subjective effort venturing the leap into faith. In this
continuing reflection—a process which is not so much articulated as experienced—the only constant factor is the uncertainty itself, which it is impossible to ignore since it is felt to be
rooted in the conscience.

The phrase 'the death of God' is meant to give theological
expression to these changed psychosocial conditions. It points
to the experience of the end of all immediate certainty, whether
objective and universal or subjective and private. Those who
remain within the scope of this new experience of the death of
God cannot escape the 'infinite pain', as Hegel called it, 'the
feeling on which the religion of the new era rests, the feeling that
God Himself is dead,[1]

In face of this experience, what point is there in seeking man's
identity and the kingdom of identity for all men? Surely this
experience of the death of God necessarily means the end of
what Jesus set himself to do? If God is dead, Jesus ceases to
concern us. Or is it perhaps the case that this very experience
forces us to seek a new and more accurate description of the
identity established in Christ? If so, what is needed is to find
other names for Christ which may be better suited to define his
work in the world.

Even as recently as the eighteenth century men were not
afraid to find new names for Christ and to give fresh currency
to old and already familiar ones. They began to use hitherto

[1] G. W. F. Hegel, *Sämtliche Werke*, ed. Lasson, Vol. I, p. 344.

unfamiliar or little used titles such as Friend, Teacher, Physician Advocate, Founder—peaceful, civilized titles after a long period dominated by terms like Hero and Warrior. But with the passing of the bourgeois period, these titles—the most recent of any importance in the history of thought—fell increasingly into disuse. Theology ceased to be aware that even today Christ could still be the Friend and Advocate, the Physician and Teacher. Older concepts were once more pressed into service to express the significance of Christ for Christians. Men again spoke, or went on speaking, of Christ as King and Lord, Shepherd and Redeemer: pictorial terms to which historical distance lent enchantment and whose very lack of immediacy seemed to promise protection against criticism and decay. At a time when the real difficulties of translating the faith from a completely vanished age into our modern period were increasing, the theologians—like the priests in the old Jerusalem temple—put back into circulation for special religious purposes a sacred coinage long since discarded. Current secular terms, which might have been used to denote Christ, had no business in the temple. Fresh designations did not emerge.

In this essay we propose to re-examine one of the oldest titles of Christ, the title of Representative. This too has become unfamiliar and almost unintelligible, having lost the concreteness it once had in salvation history. Its linguistic advantage is that it is more abstract than titles like King and Lord, that it is not already appropriated and filled out with images. It seemed easier therefore to take up this term again and to test the weight of meaning it will bear in an age very different in outlook. A more serious objection to the use of such an old term as 'representation' is that in the course of dogmatic history it has been overloaded and is already in danger of collapsing under the weight. The doctrine of representation has a specific place in dogmatics, being included among the Church's traditional statements about the office and work of Christ. It is dealt with in the context of the doctrine of the restoration of communion with God in Jesus Christ (*De fraterna redemptione*) under the rubric of Christ's

mediatorial office. On the basis of certain elements in the salvation history, this office is divided into three aspects. Just as in
the Old Testament, God's will is carried out by prophets,
priests, and kings, so Christ's office is executed in a threefold
activity (*munus triplex*). In his prophetic office Christ bears wit-
ness to salvation by his teaching; in his priestly office he achieves
salvation by his atoning sacrifice; and in his kingly office he
enters into possession of salvation in his kingdom. It is within
the doctrine of Christ's priestly office (*munus sacerdotale*) that the
doctrine of Christ's representation is dealt with. Christ died for
our sins in our stead. Representatively he reconciled us to God
and revealed God's prevenient grace towards us. If, despite this
overloading of the term representative with largely moribund
formulas which no longer awaken any response in us, we nevertheless attempt here a new 'doctrine of representation'—one
which will keep constantly in view the new conditions briefly
indicated by the term 'post-theistic'—the justification for making such an attempt is provided by the obvious difficulties in
which theology finds itself today. These difficulties are connected closely with whichever view happens to be taken in
theology of the historical process. What Christ does for man is
interpreted in accordance with one or other of two divergent
schools of thought about history. On the one hand, history is
regarded as the preordained course of what has already been
given and manifested in Christ, namely, of God's self revelation.
Christ then is seen as the 'Redeemer' (even where the term itself
is not employed), who has freed us from the various forms of
bondage which the world and society can continue to inflict on
us; he has released us, liberated us—the prisoners—by an act
thought of as archetypal and mythical. But the moment there
is no longer anything at stake in history, the moment history
vanishes into a superior salvation history with its streams of
grace invading history vertically from above, the thought of
Christ's already established sovereignty overrides the thought
of his as yet unfulfilled future.

Another way of reflecting upon and interpreting what Christ

does for us is to begin with the historicity of the person who is made possible by Christ and through him has arrived at the truth about himself. Christ then is seen as the 'firstborn among many brethren' who, in keeping with the strongly marked ethical tenor of this line of thought, has liberated us in order that we should assume responsibility for the world.

Both these interpretations of Christ's work, redemption as a *datum* of salvation history and responsibility as *historicity*, leave their mark on the possible approaches to christology, according to the varying degree of importance attached to them. The difficulty is to relate the two aspects, although of course they are inseparably linked in the Christian life. Is the relationship an irreversible sequence? What is the relation between responsibility and redemption? Is the mythical act merely the clothing of an ethical idea? How is the Redeemer related to the Rabbi who taught a higher righteousness?

Both redemption and responsibility are part of the meaning of representation. But representation itself raises these conflicting elements into a new unity. The figure of the Representative is more 'mythical' than the enlightened minds of the merely responsible allow them to imagine; and he is ethical in a sense different from that which the self-assurance of the redeemed who stand under the 'sovereignty' of Christ are prepared to admit. For he simply *represents* the kingdom of identity and joy and laughter, and does not establish it as a superior reality.

But what precisely is representation? This concept can only be used to describe the work of Jesus if it is firmly rooted in human relationships in society—in other words, only if it matches a universal phenomenon in our world as well.

We shall therefore begin in *Part I, A Provisional Interpretation*, by inquiring into ordinary current linguistic usage and shifts in meaning; then seek to describe the phenomenon of representation, and to illustrate its structures from a sociological and anthropological standpoint. The main problem which presents itself in this preliminary reflection is the idea that the individual is irreplaceable, a now generally accepted notion first formulated in German idealism. In this first part, therefore, our main discussion will be with idealist philosophy on the one hand, and positivism on the other. In *Part II*—which readers not already trained in theology can simply skip—we turn to the history of theology and examine the different views of representation found there, taking a few typical examples and of course making use of the structures uncovered in *Part I* as a critical standard. Finally, in *Part III*, we shall consider the place which the concept of representation might have within a contemporary theology. Here the problem will be christology; the fact that the man of God represents us before God and God among us, and the manner of that representation.

PART ONE

REPRESENTATION AND SUBSTITUTION
A Provisional Interpretation

'The essence of the Spirit is freedom. Its goal in the historical process is thereby given—the freedom of the subject, freedom to have its conscience and its morality, freedom to have its own universal goals and to give effect to them, freedom to have infinite value and to become aware of this ultimacy.'[1]

[1] G. W. F. Hegel, *Sämtliche Werke*, ed. Lasson, Vol. VIII, p. 426.

I

A LINGUISTIC INQUIRY

WANTING TO GO on leave, I looked for someone to represent me. When I fell ill, I had to be represented. When I died, I was replaced. Who am I? Am I replaceable? Unique? Representable? Once when I was unfit for work for a long time, a deputy came and proved more capable than me . . . On returning to work I was given another post, my incompetence having been noted. The person who should have kept my place open for me had in fact replaced me. The representative became a substitute.

Even where this happens less obviously, a similar change of attitude is surely indicated by a changing use of language. For example, the term 'replacement' (*Ersatzmann*), current during the war, ousted the older term 'reservist' (*Stellvertreter*). A corresponding linguistic development is observable in the gradual detachment of the representative (*Vertreter*) from any personal connection with those he represents. The man who once represented the head of the firm and later the firm, today represents the firm's product. The older meaning of representative, which concerns us here, has almost completely given way in current usage to its modern meaning of a commercial calling. Again, one of the rare 'loan words' adopted from German into French in the present century is the word *Ersatz* (French, *le ersatz*), there being no equivalent French word for something regarded with distaste as typically German. And while the substitute material which replaced rubber, wool or leather during the Second World War is now designated more precisely as *Kunststoff* (artificial or synthetic material), the notion of *ersatz* or substitute, has made up for this by extending its meaning, with the result that the distinction between representation and substitution tends to disappear from a current linguistic usage which has become insensitive to it. What precisely is the distinction?

To represent someone means to take responsibility for him temporarily, while he is on leave or ill. It is regarded as a temporary expedient. It is also limited to specific areas. You can represent someone in business, in an association or union, in relation to his children. To represent someone means therefore to assume conditional responsibility for him, in the hope that one's decisions will meet with his approval; it being understood that the person represented may subsequently change what the representative did in the belief that it was what the one represented would have done himself. A representative never forgets that his intervention in my place is only temporary, and that he does not permanently occupy that place. An advocate represents my interests in court, but he does not replace me. My decision to tell the truth or to remain silent, my detailed knowledge of the case, are still all-important. A representative does not put himself in the other person's place completely and absolutely. He plays a role and can play it well, but he has to realize that it is in fact a role. He appears, and makes it clear that he appears, on behalf of and in the name of the other person. He administers my property but I remain the proprietor. He knows I am irreplaceable, if only because I shall return from leave or get well again. But even if the person he represents should never return, the genuine representative never becomes a replacement. A guardian does not replace the father, he simply represents him. A foster mother is not a substitute for the dead mother, only her representative. She knows that what she does, though necessary and indeed the best that can be done in the circumstances, is not the complete, perfect and authentic thing. She does not eliminate the children's grief for their dead mother, even though she tries to help them sublimate it. She does not try to erase the mother's image from their minds; indeed, she

20

does not want them to forget her. The capacity to remember is essential to representation as a temporary, conditional, and incomplete act. It is substitution, rather, which demands oblivion. Anyone who replaces me treats me as dead.

In substitution, what is replaced is treated as unavailable, useless, or dead. Substitution demands permanence, not a merely provisional status. The replacement represents the other person completely and unconditionally. He acts in his own name, not in the name of the one he replaces. What is replaced is dead; it no longer has a name, no one remembers it. It is dead, not in the way a man who once lived and has died is dead, but as a thing is dead, inert and fixed once and for all in its particularity. The substitutionary way of thinking, for all its concreteness and definiteness, abstracts from being-in-time, and by speaking of man as a replacement turns him into a thing.

What is represented is not a dead thing but someone who is alive, who happens for the moment to be unavailable, or ill, or incapacitated, or, whatever the reason, is inactive or incapable. Representation keeps alive the memory of this living person, so that even the dead can be represented as long as men still remember them. There is a vindication of the dead in the truth they affirmed and sought in their lives and even in the truth for which they were killed and betrayed. This representative, commemorative identification with the truth sought (for the most part in vain) by the dead, is decisive for the present and the future of those now living. At the same time it also leaves room for a future for the dead themselves. Representation makes a future possible for those executed following the attempt on Hitler's life on July 20, 1944, and for the troops frozen to death at Stalingrad. What makes a future possible here is remembrance. Representation is only conceivable in the context of temporality —a temporality which can take the ontological form of weakness, immaturity, absence, or sickness. To this extent, representation safeguards the sense of history, both by remembrance and by making it possible. For however permanent and complete substitution appears to be, the fact is that discontinuity is characteristic of this world of the replaceable. The replacement can at any time itself be replaced, smoothly and without difficulty. The temporal character of representation is matched by the characteristic timelessness and indifference to time of substitution.

The disappearance of the distinction between representation and substitution from current linguistic usage is therefore indicative of the existence of a depersonalized world in which things and persons can be arbitrarily interchanged. The loss of the dimension of time is one mark of this depersonalization.

In a short poem of 1907,[1] Richard Dehmel described this depersonalized world in a recurring formula which points to the one missing yet indispensable factor: 'Only time! Only time!' Dehmel had in mind the condition of the working classes in late capitalist society, a condition that is to say of utter poverty. 'We have a bed, we have a child . . .' The only thing lacking was in fact and very concretely—time. This lack of time is attacked in the poem as an impoverishment of life as a whole. Half a century later this lack of time has become so obvious as hardly to be noticed any more. Shorter working hours tend to conceal this deprivation of time. 'Time' is lacking today, but in a different way. It is available, but the depersonalized consciousness is not in a position to use it. Such consciousness has room for neither remembrance nor a future. The lack of time, concealed under the appearance of availability, takes the form of exchangeability: Tuesday can be exchanged for Thursday, Saturday for Sunday, job for job, man for man. People whose time can be exchanged are themselves replaceable.

In fact of so massive a threat, it seems easy to answer the question posed in the opening paragraph—Am I replaceable or unique?—by roundly affirming that man is irreplaceable. This view is one of the almost self-evident principles of Western Christian thought. To deny it would seem a betrayal of human dignity. This particular individual with his frailties, excellences,

[1] The poem *Der Arbeitsmann* in Richard Dehmel, *Gesammelte Werke*, S. Fischer Verlag, Berlin 1913, Vol. I, p. 159.

and habits is unique, and so long as he lives he is irreplaceable. This theory of the irreplaceable individual is particularly in evidence when we have in view the Eastern world. We no longer ask if the individual can be represented because we take it for granted that he cannot be replaced. For substitution is a final exchange of dead impersonal or depersonalized being, whereas representation is the provisional intervention of persons on behalf of persons.

2

THE DIALECTIC OF THE ROLE

CERTAINLY THERE HAS never been in the Western tradition
any unalterable and uniform understanding of the irreplaceability of the individual. What is the basis of this irreplaceability? What necessarily distinguishes the individual from a
thing which in given circumstances can be replaced? What do
we mean when we describe the individual as a 'person', in the
modern sense of the term, as one whose identity cannot simply
be assumed as self-evident? Put simply though not inaccurately,
there are two possible explanations of man's personal being:
the traditional religious or metaphysical explanation, basing
itself on man's relation to God and regarding man as a 'soul'
in a non-psychological sense; and the modern, post-religious
explanation, basing itself on man's achievement and regarding
identity as the fruit of action setting itself to work. We can
illustrate the dividing line between these two stages—that
dominated by the metaphysical outlook and that which under-
stands identity in terms of achievement—by considering the
old conception of the *theatrum mundi*, which appears, for example,
in the plays and pageants of Calderon[1] and more recently in the
work of Hofmannsthal.[2] God was considered to be the producer
of the world drama, assigning the various roles. It is he who
makes the beggar a beggar, the king a king. It is he who
delivers Faust into the hands of Mephistopheles, just as Job was
handed over to Satan. The fact that the roles are assigned and
that human life means the playing of a part was not, however,

[1] Pedro Calderon de la Barca, Spanish dramatist, 1600-1681. One of his works
was entitled *Das grosse Welttheater* (The Great World Theatre).
[2] Hugo von Hofmannsthal, Austrian poet, 1874-1929.

felt to reduce the status of the individual. On the contrary, the splendour and profundity of the world drama derive from the very fact that it is God's drama, God's self-revelation, *theatrum Dei*. Precisely by playing a part, the individual is irreplaceable. Although a different role might have been assigned to him, he is now irrevocably engaged to play this particular part. Any suggestion of miscasting by this producer is automatically ruled out. No-one can escape from his role in the world theatre or strip off the costume issued to him. From the standpoint of the world, the terms of the engagement permit no dissociation from the role once the player is on stage.

Yet even within the terms of this conception, the individual is allowed a certain measure of dissociation from his role. But only in relation to God as the producer of the play: a freedom which is both preserved and hidden in Him. The 'I' behind the role makes no appearance on stage, in the world. Nor is there any need for this 'I' to appear, since God, who alone assigns the roles, knows that a distinction must be made between the 'I' and the role it plays. On stage, in the world, empirically, the 'I' vanishes into its role, but the intelligible 'I' remains safe and secure in God's remembrance. It is only in respect of this inalienable core—in traditional Christian language, only in respect of the 'soul'—that the individual is irreplaceable. God does not judge him by the role he plays, in the manner of some naive, ignorant spectator. What really matters is not the social or even the moral status of the role in question, since God the producer takes responsibility for this and asks only whether, within its limits, the individual has fully exploited the role's possibilities or wasted them. His concern is simply with the way the soul conducts and proves itself, in the costume of the role in question.

In relation to our question about the irreplaceable individual, this means that we cannot explain man's irreplaceability in terms of a psychologically demonstrable uniqueness, determinable by reference to a man's life. If identity is safe in heaven, earthly non-identity can be endured. A dialectic of the role arises, a tension between this dissociation from the role and engagement in it. However much the actor is engaged in the playing of his role, a certain detachment from it remains because he knows that the role now assigned to him does not fully express him. This dialectic of the role contains a qualified answer to the introductory question about the irreplaceable individual, an answer which will occupy our attention later. As one who plays a role in God's drama, I am always both irreplaceable and yet able to be represented.

In the course of the expanding process of secularization, the metaphysical irreplaceability of the human soul was itself transposed into secular language and explained in terms of certain achievements or expressions of life by which the individual made himself irreplaceable. Man discovered himself as essentially one who accomplishes things, and this prospect of self-realization, self-accomplishment, self-expression in work, blotted out the earlier metaphysical horizon. Now for the first time, in the context of the modern discovery of the individual, it was a man's work—labour performed, his perfected achievement—which merited the dignity and status given to the relation between producer and player in the earlier conception. Man no longer acquired his identity simply from his relationship to God, which had once in itself provided an adequate explanation of the irreplaceability of the individual as a soul. He now achieves his own identity; he makes himself irreplaceable.

This new basis which the self creates by its own efforts can no longer find support in the symbol of the *theatrum mundi*. To play a role is now felt to be depersonalizing. Indeed, one who lives on the basis of this new self-achieved irreplaceability is bound to regard the old symbol as a menacing spectre. The transition is typified by Jacques in Shakespeare's *As You Like It* when he describes with extreme detachment the theatrical character of human life as a whole:

> All the world's a stage
> And all the men and women merely players.
> They have their exits and their entrances,

The Dialectic of the Role

And one man in his time plays many parts,
His acts being seven ages.[1]

The drama played in the *theatrum mundi* has lost its seriousness. The sceptic sees through it and muses ironically on it. Playing a part now implies man's complete replaceability. But whereas in Shakespeare the scepticism is still hesitant, still undecided whether the symbol is meaningful or meaningless, the symbol gradually deteriorates until it becomes the symbol *par excellence* for fate and in the end for absurdity. Sceptical detachment turns into scorn for the producer. In the early romantic novel *The Vigil of Bonaventura*,[2] God appears as an incompetent *régisseur* who stages his insipid production in an improvised theatre with a cast of provincial players. The 'role' now becomes the term for complete interchangeability and finds a new expression in the scepticism, futility and nihilism which have always moved below the surface of bourgeois idealist thought from its very beginnings. Hitherto interpreted dialectically as the tension between engagement in this world and an accompanying detachment vested in the producer, the term 'role' now becomes undialectical and patent of one interpretation only. The essentially representative nature of the role disappears and the role becomes the symbol of replaceability. The decisive thing now is not that the role is 'assigned' but that it demonstrates that man is replaceable.

For whenever the individual imagines that he is unmistakable and unique, society puts him right and instructs him about exchangeability.

Long, long ago, a green beginner
I thought myself a special case.

(None of your ordinary run of the mill girls, with my looks and my talent and my love of higher things.)[3]

This song, which tells of the experience of exchangeability,

[1] *Act* II, Sc. 7.
[2] An anonymous German novel of 1805.
[3] Bertolt Brecht, *Mother Courage*.

27

Brecht calls 'The Song of the Great Capitulation'! The claim to be unique is disallowed. The triviality of the ordinary carries the day. The ostensibly spontaneous life of the individual is shown to be the playing of a role, inextricably interwoven with other roles which are all essentially predetermined. The claim of the individual to be a 'special case' is countered by a society which provides qualities and attitudes for every conceivable situation. In this clash, society proves more than a match for the 'special' individual, for its claims cannot be evaded by him with impunity. Indeed, society assigns certain prefabricated roles to the individual long before he even notices the extent to which he, the unique and irreplaceable individual, is its prisoner.

We cannot take a single step, utter a single word, without the intervention of a third party between ourselves and the world, binding us to the world and mediating between these two extremely concrete abstractions, namely society.[1]

Society makes claims on the occupants of certain positions, and these claims are in fact their roles within society.[2] They are assigned to the player in advance and he must learn them so as to master them. They consist of a complex of behaviour patterns which, along with other behaviour patterns, constitute a whole of which they form a 'part'—which is another word for 'role' in English and French. Finally, from the standpoint of the player, they are, as roles, in no sense exhaustive. He could always play other roles, too. Nor is he completely tied to the one now assigned to him, as was the case in the *theatrum mundi* where, in keeping with the static social order of a pre-industrial age, the role was more fixed and at the same time linked with a greater freedom to improvise. Ordinarily, the individual had the same role for life, whereas present day mobility encourages the change of roles. Yet the roles of the earlier period did permit the individual more freedom of movement, as can be seen for example in the dramatic pieces of the seventeenth century

---

[1] Ralf Dahrendorf, *Homo sociologicus, Ein Versuch zur Geschichte, Bedeutung und Kritik der sozialen Rollen*, Köln, 1961, p. 10.
[2] *Ibid.*, p. 22.

Spanish writer, Calderon. Although assigned one particular role for life, the individual was far less restricted than he is in most of the roles provided and imposed by modern society.

The process of man's socialization gathers momentum; and this socialization, and the imposition and fixing of roles which accompanies it, could by its very character rob the individual of any belief in himself as a 'special case', were it not that an all-pervasive propaganda, encouraging him in such belief, successfully conceals from the individual consciousness his actual condition of interchangeability. At the same time, the dialectic of the role, still preserved in the older conception, in which engagement and detachment confirmed each other in tension, now disappears. Henceforth, engagement in the role, and detachment from it, are both diminished and the metaphor of spare parts in a machine seems more apt than that of parts in a play.

In the *theatrum mundi* interpretation, the individual's detachment from his role meant simply that he was aware that his role was a temporary and transient performance. The player represented a particular calling; he was not identified with it. This awareness secured for the individual a space beyond his deeds, making it possible for him to withdraw from everything chargeable to individual responsibility. We still find in Lessing the astonishing appeal to the God

> Who alone does not need
> To judge man by his deeds
> Which so seldom are his own deeds, O God.[1]

But this dissociation from the role, based upon man's relationship to God, can only be secularized by assuming the utter irresponsibility of all human action—by escaping into a purely aesthetic, non-involved existence, as is always possible and tolerated.

The older concept of engagement in a role which had to be played as completely and as effectively as possible while life

[1] Lessing, *Nathan the Wise*, V, 4.

lasted, has become, in the modern situation (where roles are exchanged), a short-term, occasional adaptation. As the concept of detachment from the role was secularized, the degree of engagement in the role was also reduced. The term 'role' was increasingly interpreted non-dialectically. The player became a replaceable substitute, and to take on a role became merely a matter of adapting oneself to an interchangeability clearly taken for granted.

3

THE IDEALIST THESIS—
THE IRREPLACEABLE INDIVIDUAL

THIS REINTERPRETATION OF the idea of the role, changing it from a divine task giving dignity and irreplaceability to the individual into a hollow symbol of his replaceability, was not accepted without opposition, of course. The role-concept contains the idea that the individual is replaceable but it also continues to imply a definite criticism of the idea that all are alike interchangeable. From the actor's standpoint no particular role can be exhaustive. Even a part specially written for him does not completely and inevitably express him. However well suited he may be for the kind of roles he is expected to play, no individual can be content to accept a role which may perhaps also be closely drawn and leave little room for improvisation, any more than an actor can be content to be completely identified with one particular role he plays. There is a yearning for identity which, once kindled and expressed, can never again be quenched.

This yearning is nourished by an innate knowledge of identity, however fragmentary, such as we experience, for example, in recollections of childhood, in the presence of answered love, in the hope of tolerable human conditions. Such experiences remind us of ourselves and assure us of our irreplaceability, in spite of the existence of a depersonalized world in which exchange and substitution is the general rule.

Historically, this consciousness of the irreplaceability of the individual emerged and was formulated at the time when the idea of the role became the favourite symbol of meaninglessness:

that is to say in the period of German idealism. The more the 'I' felt itself to be playing a part, the more it realized that it was as helpless and replaceable as, in Werther's words 'a puppet moved by hidden strings'. (This was particularly the case in the German situation where the rising middle classes found little scope for life and work and independent responsibility.) And as this happened, the more clearly did the awareness of irreplaceability, which is so intimately bound up with the question of personal identity, emerge in the philosophy in which human self-consciousness expresses itself. If in what follows we limit our attention to Hegel, it is because in this matter otherwise important differences between the various idealist systems can be disregarded.

Writing about the fall of man which, he says, made man aware of his freedom, Hegel declares that here we can see man's

infinite being-for-self, which did not thus come into consciousness in the earlier religions, in which the contrast or opposition did not go as far as this absolute stage, nor attain to this depth. Because this happened here, man's worth is immediately put on a much higher level. The subject has hereby acquired absolute importance; it is essentially an object of interest to God, since it is self-consciousness existing for itself.[1]

What is the basis of this sense of absolute importance of the subject and what sustains the sense of irreplaceable uniqueness inseparable from it? Hegel answers that God is interested in the subject and that this makes it impossible for the subject to renounce its own identity.

Hegel here stands within the Western tradition which stated man's longing for irreplaceability in metaphysical terms. It is as a soul that the individual is regarded as irreplaceable: what can be said of his inexchangeable irreplaceability depends on the soul, which lives in direct relationship with God. God is the soul's home, its 'true country', as Augustine, faithful to the

[1] G. W. F. Hegel, *Philosophie der Religion*, ed. Glockner, Vol. 16, p. 267f. See ET in *Lectures on the Philosophy of Religion*, tr. E. B. Speirs and J. B. Sanderson, London 1895, Vol. 3, p. 56.

Platonist tradition, affirmed. 'God and the soul, that is what I desire to know. Nothing more? Nothing whatever.'[1] In his *On the Measure of the Soul*, Augustine actually defines the soul as that which is for God 'the pure neighbour'.[2] It is 'like' God although as a creature quite distinct from him. Metaphysical assertions of this kind are the ontological basis which explains why the individual is irreplaceable, even in the world and in his own sight. In this knowledge, of 'God and the soul . . . nothing more', the irreplaceability of the individual is secure.

There may be other forms of identity, originating in non-European traditions for example, for which the irreplaceability of the individual is not indispensable. But the Western tradition cannot break this law it has inherited, that identity always implies irreplaceable and non-exchangeable being. Because this identity is not given in advance, but set as a task (and that means always at the same time lost), it is all the more urgently in need of another outside itself if it is to be recovered or attained. That is to say, it cannot be a self-contained substance which could be thought of as analogous to natural reality, but only as a definite relationship—entered into or refused—which is the basis of personal identity in the world. Identity is only realized in relation to others or to the 'idea'. Man's irreplaceability rests on 'God's interest' in him and not on the richness, profundity or divine likeness of his soul. In other words, identity is always an achievement, not something I assume or think. Certainly it is also possible to use the soul's likeness to God to interpret man's uniqueness in natural, substantial terms, as was done after Augustine. But the ontological basis of irreplaceability is not the substance of the 'soul'. In the beginning was—the relationship! Irreplaceability presupposes a standing-in-relationship. Man cannot be thought of as a self-sufficient being. Identity is not achieved independently: it is not something available to, or attainable by, the individual as such. No one

---

[1] Augustine, *Soliloquies* Bk. I sec. 7 in *Nicene and Post Nicene Fathers*, Ist Ser., Vol. VII, p. 539.
[2] Augustine, *De quantitate animae*, Migne, 32, I, 1073f.

can make himself irreplaceable. For all that, the danger of falling into this misinterpretation in terms of substance (mistaking irreplaceability for a substance and therefore dehistoricizing it and detaching it from personal relationship) was especially acute for the very people who right at the beginning of the idealist period recognized the threat of exchangeability and opposed it.

Here, too, Hegel marked a culminating point at which the loftiness of thought is achieved only at the price of extreme vulnerability. Still dominated by traditional theology, he claimed 'God's interest' in the 'absolute importance of the subject'. But, as the founder of modern social philosophy, he also knew that the individual wants to be recognized and to secure confirmation of his personal irreplaceability; and that he can only do so by devoting himself to things—in other words by work. Hegel therefore consistently interprets irreplaceability as a relational concept, but one with a twofold reference, to God and to society. As infinite worth and absolute importance, the subject's irreplaceable being is guaranteed only by God; but as earthly existence, losing and finding itself again in work, it is autonomous being-for-itself which is operative. Substance and relationship fuse in what Hegel calls 'the Spirit', and the infinite worth is both given in advance and set as a task. With typical ambivalence, 'God's interest' is manifested in the alienation of work, and being-for-itself remains ambiguously both achievement and grace.

The polemic conducted by the dialectic theologians against German idealism completely missed the mark. It is just not true that German idealism celebrated and glorified man's autonomy. What in fact Hegel did was to reflect theologically on man's work. It is no accident that the two fundamental ideas which he regarded as the basis of man's irreplaceability were illustrated by Hegel from the story of man's fall. On the one hand, 'God's interest' which, in order to be able to love, requires 'differentiation and the removal of the difference'; on the other, the work of man, who alienates himself and 'must make himself what he is'.[1] These two things—man's differentiated relationship to God and his achievement—must be seen as a dialectical unity. For Hegel, identity is only made possible by alienation, by work. Only by the negation of itself does identity find itself: as oneness in differentiation, as identity in non-identity.

It could even be said that work, as the essential characteristic of the Spirit, is in fact the very thing which interests God in man. As one who works, one who exists-for-himself, one who has been driven from the paradise of pure identity and is henceforth irrevocably differentiated from God: such a man is of 'interest' to God; in his alienation man acquires 'absolute importance'. So long as man was still in paradise, this absolute importance was unnecessary. For it formed no part of his natural equipment, but rather it constitutes his history as the differentiation which is recognized and removed by God. According to Hegel, 'the differentiation and the removal of the difference' is the 'love' which alone makes identity possible and establishes it.

When we say God is love, we are expressing a very great and true thought, but it would be unreasonable to take this in so simple a way as a simple characterization of God without analysing the meaning of love. For love implies a distinguishing between two and yet these two are in fact not distinguished from one another. Love, this feeling of being outside myself, is the feeling and consciousness of this identity. My self-consciousness is not in myself but in another; but this other, in whom I alone find satisfaction and am at peace with myself—and I exist only insofar as I am at peace with myself, for if I had not this inner peace I would be the contradiction which falls apart—this other, just because it is outside of me, has its self-consciousness only in me. Thus the two are represented simply by this consciousness of their being outside themselves and of their identity, and this perception, this feeling, this knowledge of the unity is love, and it is idle talk to speak of love unless we know that it is the differentiation and the removal of the difference.[2]

Soon after Hegel, the theological and sociological aspects of

---

[1] G. W. F. Hegel, *Philosophie der Religion*, ed. Glockner, Vol. 16, p. 267. Cf. ET Speirs and Sanderson, Vol. 3, pp. 55f.

[2] G. W. F. Hegel, *Philosophie der Religion*, ed. Lasson, Vol. XIV, p. 75. Cf. ET Speirs and Sanderson, Vol. 3, p. 10.

the matter fell apart. The irreplaceable man and his identity continue of course to be important themes, but the explanations given of them are now very various.

To illustrate this we turn to the work of Adolf von Harnack, one of the later representatives of German idealism. He too declares that man is irreplaceable. But the 'infinite value of the human soul', the heart of the Gospel proclaimed by Jesus, is not regarded by Harnack as *within* man's relation to God but as *prior* to it, and therefore interpreted in terms of substance. 'God as the Father, and the human soul so ennobled that it can and does unite with Him'—these are the 'restful and restgiving notes in the message of Jesus'.[1] 'But Jesus Christ was the first to bring the value of each human soul to light, and what he did no one can any more undo.'[2] 'Human lives, we ourselves, have become dearer to one another.'[3] For Harnack, the subject of this relation between God and the soul is the 'soul' which 'can unite with Him'. The basis of its infinite worth is its 'nobility'; surely a substance concept, even if the nobility was originally a gift. Irreplaceability is here regarded as something natural; the nobility is given in advance and does not have still to be proved in alienation. Harnack's account of this nobility completely ignores the question how the individual can achieve identity in a definite and given social and historical context. In Hegel's terms, identity is presented by Harnack without 'differentiation', without 'work', and without 'non-identity'. So it is in fact 'idle talk' when Harnack says: 'Jesus Christ calls to every poor soul' (unlike Plato who reserved his praise for the infinite value of the knowing mind), 'he calls to everyone who bears a human face: "You are children of the living God, and not only better than many sparrows but of more value than the whole world" '.[4] Identity here is neither an achievement nor an experienced event, nor is it the Hegelian dialectical unity of the two, but simply a gracious fact. Thus Harnack involuntarily slips into an interpretation of 'infinite value' which leads further and further

[1] Adolf von Harnack, *What is Christianity?* ET T. B. Saunders, London, 1901 (Harper Torchbooks 1957), p. 63.
[2] *Ibid.*, p. 67f.   [3] *Ibid.*, p. 70.   [4] *Op. cit.*, p. 67.

away from 'God's interest' in man, and, despite intentions to the contrary, the value of the soul can now be understood as its profundity, its qualities, its capacities—in short, as inwardness. With the abandonment of the outward, the subject's absolute importance now becomes the value of the 'soul' in the modern psychological sense. A case in point is the well-known mistranslation (and misinterpretation) of the New Testament verse: 'What shall it profit a man if he gain the whole world and lose his own soul?'—where for 'soul' we should read 'life', as the New Testament intended.

Far more important than this interiorizing theological view of the irreplaceable man, of course, is the other view which follows the lead given by the socio-philosophical aspect of Hegel's thought and finds the basis of man's irreplaceability in his performance. In particular demands, situations and even misfortunes, man discovers by experience that he is irreplaceable. Here—whether in conflict, in exceptional individual performance, or unique individual misfortune—the individual achieves identity because he cannot be replaced. Schiller makes his soldiers in *Wallenstein's Camp* celebrate their calling in these terms:

> No help to him there by another is shown
> He stands for himself and himself alone.[1]

Such soldierly feeling derives its force precisely from the idea of the irreplaceable man who cannot be represented. The decisive moments in life, these heroic manly voices assert, are the moments when you cannot be replaced, when no one else can represent you. To this way of thinking, representation has no meaning except for those who are inadequate. German idealism did not invent this idea, of course. Every version of heroic thought, from the German saga right down to Ernst Jünger, insists on man's non-representability and assumes his self-sufficiency. Man stands for himself and himself alone. Irre-

[1] ET by James Churchill in *The Works of Frederick Schiller*, London, 1846, Vol. 2, p. 174.

placeability is clearly equated here with non-representability. The same applies to the kind of irreplaceability which expresses itself not so much in heroic demonstration as in accomplished work, in that creative 'self-begetting act of man' by man,[1] which establishes identity. Who then still guarantees the individual his irreplaceability?

What once God had guaranteed had needed no worldly authentication. To be irreplaceable for God was enough. In every other relationship one could continue to play a particular role in society without claiming uniqueness, and without feeling degraded as a person by being exchangeable. Modern thought could be classified according to new guarantees of irreplaceability which have been suggested from time to time: Love, Fatherland, Art, Work, and so on—merely to give the broad outlines. All these have been employed to confirm the thesis, derived from the Christian tradition and in need of worldly authentication: the thesis that man is irreplaceable.

[1] Karl Marx, *Jugendschriften*, ed. S. Landshut, 1953, p. 281.

4

THE ANTITHESIS—
EVERYTHING IS INTERCHANGEABLE

BUT THE WORLD we live in—'in' not in the way a cup happens to be 'in' the cupboard but could equally well be elsewhere—gives the lie to all fine talk about the irreplaceable individual. Indeed the world wrings from us a profound feeling that, on the contrary, everything is interchangeable. When we are looking for work, there are always a great many other applicants with the same qualifications. Human situations which to us may seem quite unique and unmistakable can be traced back by any psychologist to their typical prototypes and matched with the standard available solutions. But the thesis that man is irreplaceable is open to attack, and not only from the standpoint of social psychology. It is equally vulnerable, if not more so, when we consider the nature of our human products, the material basis of our life. Every object we produce and use to-day exists in a multitude of identical copies, all exactly alike in every physical respect. Mechanical methods of mass production make all objects interchangeable. The accidental and the imperfect, which constitute much of the charm of hand-made objects, lose their appeal, just as the history which an object may have had also loses its interest once everything can be re-created. The house in which Goethe was born in Frankfurt, and which was destroyed during the Second World War, was completely reconstructed and restored as if nothing had happened. Even the vanished past can be recreated, providing the technical conditions for the reproduction of each object are satisfied. The methods evolved by mass production for marketing, ad-

39

vertising, and distributing what is produced go one step further in depriving the products of their individual character, their historical and geographical particularity. As Walter Benjamin says, they lose their 'aura', and are regarded as 'wares', or 'goods'; as capital investment to be bought and sold, or (in certain social groups) as status symbols. No account can be taken here of the objects themselves as something tangible and particular.

The world which has emerged with these saleable mass-produced goods, a world which is replaceable down to the last detail, leads the individual to regard himself too as a replaceable part in a machine. The contemporary sense of futility is in great measure connected with this interchangeability. What is disturbing is not that the individual is simply a part of, or simply plays a role in, a larger whole, for even parts can be irreplaceable. For example, in an organism, each part is essential for the whole: a concept revived and developed in German idealism by Herder, Goethe, and Humboldt. Though its functions may be clearly demarcated a particular part can nevertheless temporarily assume the functions of other parts as well. No part can be detached from the organism except in the course of a gradual process of growth, nor can it be replaced like a machine part.

But this conception of the organism and the relation of the part to the whole seems quite inapplicable today. The progressive division of labour makes the meaning of work increasingly obscure to the individual. The individual's relation to his work, his sense of 'vocation', is weakened and can even vanish altogether. Just as it makes no difference to the production process who occupies which seat at the switch-board (it is the individual's mechanical efficiency that counts, not his personal qualities), so too it is immaterial to the individual where he works. The work is the same, wherever it is. Congeniality of working conditions, and related factors, are what matter to him. Consequently, the kind of work chosen is determined by considerations unrelated to the work itself. It is not important that

I should do this work rather than that. Someone else could equally well occupy my place. Anyone who is sacked or dies is at once replaced, even the supposedly 'indispensable colleague'. The replacement of the individual researcher by the team in science, of the solitary charismatic ruler by the directing 'group' or 'top brains' in politics, brings a little closer the establishment of replaceability as the basic principle in the practice of the division of labour. This division of labour militates strongly against the individualistic idea that the individual is irreplaceable. The very existence and continuance of this practice demonstrates that the individual can in fact be replaced. Ideologists may still cling to the idea of irreplaceability, but the whole basis of life has so changed that solemn talk of such ideas at graduation ceremonies and funerals can only strike a false note.

Sensing this, the individual who has become replaceable clings all the more anxiously to his supposed irreplaceability and tries to *be* unique. He develops a 'personal style', adopts a distinctive manner and appearance, pursues his personal hobbies, often without noticing that even these badges of individuality have long been commercially planned, encouraged, and exploited. Even the most private realm is no longer a refuge where the individual can realize his desire to be unique and distinctive. Even someone who tries to cultivate his individuality by pursuing a special hobby finds himself merely responding to the expectations of the leisure-time industry. The replaceable individual, imagining himself to be in every respect unique, endeavours to make himself so indispensable that not merely substitution but even representation of any kind seems impossible. The general manager who likes to explain, 'I can't take a holiday because things don't get done without me', imagines himself not merely irreplaceable but completely nonrepresentable too. He feels that even to be represented is tantamount to death. Representation becomes increasingly unrecognizable and unfamiliar, as the shift in linguistic usage referred to earlier showed. Substitution remains the only available category. The general manager rightly sees that substitution treats

41

the person replaced as unavailable, incapable, or dead. Unwilling to be unavailable, incapable or dead, he makes himself available everywhere and at all times, makes himself ceaselessly, and, as it were, unsleepingly alive.

When the possibility of representation is rejected, only two possibilities remain: either death or life, either to be replaced or to be irreplaceable. Between this death and a life in which one works like mad, between being replaced and being irreplaceable, between complete absence and complete presence, there is no third possibility, no mediation. This either-or thinking is perfectionistic and therefore unrealistic. For real life never presents itself in so uninterrupted, so unsleeping, so perfect a form. On the contrary, it is actually a feature of real life that we should sometimes be absent, tired, incapacitated, incapable, or ill. But such imperfect conditions are intolerable in a depersonalized world. The 'indispensable colleague' is in fact the ideological correlate of a world where everything is in practice replaceable. What still sounds well at funerals, proves an insupportable burden to the object of the tribute when alive—a law none the less deadly for having been willingly accepted. The claim that the individual is irreplaceable needs therefore to be corrected. When this claim is detached from any basis in technical, social and political conditions in the modern world, it becomes suspect as an ideology. The world which surrounds and shapes us asserts, by its very existence, the antithesis: that everyone can be replaced. But this completely altered basis of life could help us to see that man's irreplaceability—since we are determined to hold on to this—cannot be founded on man's own achievement.

5

THE SYNTHESIS—
MAN IS IRREPLACEABLE YET
REPRESENTABLE

BUT WHAT COMPELS us to cling to the bourgeois idealist thesis
that the individual is irreplaceable, when all our experience
contradicts it? The answer is: that desire for identity, which the
consciousness can never be persuaded to abandon, because of
definite historical experiences it has had of its possibility. No
change in the basis of life, however radical, can expunge certain
developed stages of consciousness as if they had never been.
'The infinite value of the human soul', praised by Harnack at
the end of the 'bourgeois century' as the discovery of the gospel,
certainly becomes an empty ideology once it is viewed in ab-
straction from social and political reality, and therefore with a
complete disregard for any possible basis. But this misuse of the
thesis does not determine its truth or falsity. The consciousness,
which has been altered and moulded by certain discoveries,
refuses to be sidetracked. Once articulated, 'no thought in any
human soul was ever lost'.[1] The thought of irreplaceability is
no exception. It cannot be withdrawn. Men can find new explanations for it, and it can be misconstrued, as crassly as it was
by the manager referred to earlier; but it cannot be eradicated.
Hegel had based human dignity and the absolute importance
of the individual on the differentiation in which the separate
individual already exists. He is separate, differentiated, firstly
from God, whose 'interest' is continually aroused by this

[1] J. G. Herder, *Über den Ursprung der menschlichen Sprache*, 1170, Part 2, Sec. 4,
Naturgesetz.

difference; and secondly from other individuals and from society, whose recognition he strives to win by work which establishes his distinction. Man thus achieves identity in a strangely ambiguous way: from God's interest and society's recognition. The question is whether this ambiguity can be resolved by choosing between these two sources.

Can the consciousness of the 'infinite value of the subject' still be maintained in a post-metaphysical period? Can man think of and experience this 'absolute importance' even apart from God's interest in him? Can he do so when it is no longer an interest he experiences, and in a post-theistic age? Can he safeguard it for others? If God is dead what meaning have words like 'absolute', 'infinite', 'irreplaceable'? If there is no longer anything unconditional to guarantee the infinite, incalculable worth of the subject, what basis can there be for a 'real humanism' such as Marx wanted? Can mankind take over God's role, as Feuerbach imagined? But this would surely mean relativizing the absolute importance of the individual and therefore making it exchangeable? Does the 'soul' so depend upon God that the death of God would inevitably involve the death of the soul too? These questions can only be raised here to show the far-reaching implications of the use of the vocable 'God' in our day. For what does it mean to assert that God is dead if, and so long as, there is still something which concerns us unconditionally? Is not atheism merely a different mode of speech from theism? Does not everything depend on anthropology, that is to say on the problem of the irreplaceable man who is seeking personal identity and can never be freed from this search? For if we regard 'God' as the One who by his 'interest' guarantees the infinite value of the subject, by the same token we can also say that this infinite value appears in the consciousness of the individual as an ineradicable claim. To realize his true identity is an essential element of man's longing.

What is experienced is not the identity but the difference between, on one hand, the possible but unattainable life (present only in the form of a claim or desire or hope) and, on the other, the experienced impossibility of living this life, in other words, the difference between identity and non-identity. But, however one deals with this experience, identity turns out to be dependence. No-one can make himself irreplaceable. If we ignore the dative case—*for whom* am I irreplaceable?—the subject suffers. To fail to ask this question is to miss the secret of the irreplaceable man, which, as will emerge later, is inseparable from the possibility of representation.

For I am never irreplaceable for those for whom I merely perform some task. The performance of a task is always characterized by a disappearance of the person into the task performed. In work, man experiences an alienation which 'removes', '*destroys*', him as pure immediacy. In work, his immediate desire is 'restrained'; the 'evanescence' or 'disappearance' of the object which the desire would consume is 'delayed and postponed'.[1] We need not reflect here upon the way in which the man who alienates himself in work recovers himself again, how he begets himself through the medium of his labour. For our present purpose it is sufficient to observe that anyone who in work alienates himself into some cause is exchangeable in his existence for others. It does not matter to the master which slave ploughs his field. What interests him is the slave's work, not his person. What matters is the capacity of the slave, not the slave himself. In this sense, everyone who performs a task is potentially replaceable. The depersonalization of man in work; the great farewell to all immediacy, as celebrated in Hegel's philosophy; mediation into the thing; the alienation of man—these are structures which make the individual seem merely a tiny replaceable part in the total process.

For those for whom I merely perform some task, I am never irreplaceable. Irreplaceability of a kind has certainly emerged in human life as lived and in its special non-repeatable groupings. Such irreplaceability proves important in a particular historical situation where one particular man alone can act and

[1] G. W. F. Hegel, *Phänomenologie des Geistes*, ed. Hoffmeister, p. 149. ET J. B. Baillie, *The Phenomenology of Mind*, 2 vols, London 1910, Vol. I, p. 186.

take the initiative. But this kind of irreplaceability—say, of some historical figure—does not derive exclusively from his contribution in isolation. At the same time it includes something more in reality and experience, shining out in the situation itself. It is indicative that this kind of irreplaceability is becoming rarer and disappearing altogether under the modern horizon so dominated by this idea of contribution. It is rooted in an attitude to history which will soon be quite anachronistic in an industrialized society characterized by a non-historicity concerned primarily with such an idea.

Whenever man's horizon is bounded by his contribution, substitution also comes into play. A different basis must be found for man's irreplaceability. I am irreplaceable only for those who love me. Only for them does a surplus remain, over and above whatever I perform at any given time: something not expressed in my action. This margin, this surplus of the person over and above all he performs, alone gives life to human relationships. To love means, in this sense, to count on this surplus, on what has not yet been expressed, not yet appeared. The invisible and unexpressed surplus is a reminder that I have not yet reached my full stature. Identity continues to be preserved in the experience of difference; in the consciousness of non-identity. But this consciousness knows that it cannot expunge itself. I do not become an irreplaceable person by my own effort, but only as I continue to be dependent on others.

I am irreplaceable for those who set their hope in me. They secure me something which is denied to all exchangeable things, namely, time. They rescue my time from that neutral interchangeability in which nothing new happens under the sun, in which each day and hour can be exchanged for another just as non-historical. The time gained for me in this way includes the possibility of remembrance and the possibility of a future.

All this presupposes that man is a being who needs representation. This dependence on representation cannot be dismissed

46

as a relapse into immaturity nor regarded as an unenlightened mythological archaism. The conception of man as a self-sufficient hero, needing no-one's help, relying on himself, irreplaceable and non-representable, whose affairs are no concern of others, is confronted by the other conception of man—man unable, today, to take responsibility for himself; aware of not being self-contained, living as he does in immaturity, incapacity, and weakness. In the heroic world, this inability to stand alone would have been a cause for despair. The hero who cannot fight, whatever the reason may be, goes under. It is either victory or defeat; no third solution is conceivable.

Not so in the case of the hero in the fairy tale, whom we introduce here by way of illustration. Confronted by impossible tasks, on which sometimes his very life depends, the fairy tale hero nevertheless is not doomed to perish tragically, since the fairy story knows of a basic category which is foreign to the saga (even to that of the manager): the category of representation. Another creature, sometimes an animal, often a human being under a spell, intervenes and acts in place of the hero, who is himself helpless and has in many cases by his own folly got himself into the impossible situation from which he now finds it impossible to extricate himself. Exhausted and in despair, convinced of the hopelessness of his situation, he falls asleep. This sleeping at a time when his life is in imminent danger; at the very last moment before he is due to die say, because he cannot find the pearl in the ocean—all this underlines the vulnerability, the defencelessness of someone who finds himself reduced by overstrain to a state of immaturity. He sleeps while another—in order to save his life—journeys, or builds, or seeks. At this very moment, the ants are gathering the scattered seeds; the fox is building the palace instead of the sleeping hero. Representation takes place here exactly as we described it earlier. The representative acts for the other person, arranges his affairs for him. But he represents him only incompletely: only in this particular situation—and only conditionally. This is expressed in the fairy tale by the fact that the hero is not rescued, once and for all.

He is given further opportunities for foolish action, he is allowed to land himself in other impossible situations. To this extent, in the fairy tale, representation is never substitution, it never treats the one who is represented as dead. It is always an open-ended action on behalf of the one who is represented. When the fox represents the sleeping, incompetent hero, he keeps his place open for him. 'Place' here is equivalent to 'life'. It never enters the representative's head to claim the deserved reward for himself; the hand of the king's daughter in marriage, for example. He really does act 'in the name' of the other and not in his own name or on his own behalf. The threat of someone usurping delegated authority (a danger that immediately occurs to minds as schooled to competition as ours) simply does not arise in this context.

Any act of representation can turn into substitution if the place of the one who is represented is no longer held open, but is seized by the representative for himself. The temptation to outshine a colleague for whom one is deputizing, by treating him as less efficient, incapable, or non-existent, is almost irresistible. Any provisional representative act can turn into a completely substitutionary act which forgets its own provisionality. It also follows that the wish to be represented is almost invariably accompanied by the fear of being replaced. For it is in most cases impossible to define representation precisely, in terms of its functions, unless we confine ourselves to the legal sense of the term, where it is essential to restrict representation to certain legal acts, such as the making of depositions. In every other use, however, there is an element of insecurity, for it is impossible to settle in advance the exact extent of the authority to represent. The risk inherent in all personal relationships becomes particularly evident in the case of representation. Anyone who is represented runs the risk of being replaced. Unwillingness to take this risk betrays many into a perfectionistic way of thinking for which it is simply a choice between being dead and being ceaselessly alive, between being replaced and being irreplaceable.

It is therefore characteristic of this perfectionistic way of thinking to oscillate fitfully between the ideology which declares euphorically that 'the individual is irreplaceable' and the disillusioning experience of a basis of life for which 'every one is replaceable'. Ideal and reality are no longer related to each other but confront one another helplessly as sterile opposites. This split-consciousness is marked by sudden conversions. Dissatisfied with the experience of complete interchangeability, the consciousness eagerly turns its back on this situation and transfers itself to the pseudo-idealist glorification of one irreplaceable individual or a superior group, an élite. When the charismatic leader or the élite proves a failure, it is not too difficult to return to the ideological position from which it began. This is why in Germany today there are in fact hardly any 'old Nazis' and a surprisingly large number of potential fascists. Easily embittered, yet fully convinced that this is the position it has always taken, the consciousness returns to its positivism now that its flirtation with irrationalism has come to grief. The irreplaceable individual has turned out to be a dream. The awakened dreamer feels it was to his credit even to have dreamed such a noble dream. In any case, it is not up to him to resolve the contradiction between the dream of the irreplaceable man and the experience of complete interchangeability. So the two live side by side in a tranquil schizophrenia. Common to both is the perfectionism which rules out a third possibility between life and death, victory and defeat, all and nothing. Both omit from their interpretation of man his essential dependence.

The contradiction between the idealist thesis that 'man is irreplaceable' and the positivist antithesis that 'each man is replaceable' cannot be resolved by choosing between them and imagining that the truth of the one can only be maintained by resolutely ignoring the truth of the other. To turn a blind eye in either direction would automatically indicate that whichever thesis one adopted was being maintained as an ideology. If, for example, we were to choose the idealist thesis, it would inevitably be an ideology which imagined itself superior to, and independent of, any basis; whereas in fact it is inescapably confronted by this basis, and at its mercy. On the other hand, to choose the positivist thesis would merely mean hypostasizing the existing structures—man's self-estrangement as a result of the division of labour, his depersonalization and loss of historicity—as if they were the only ones possible, and unalterable.

The insoluble contradiction must be endured. Everything depends on keeping this irreplaceable-replaceable man in view. But this is only possible when the contradiction, regarded as a dialectical opposition, is mediated in another, third thesis; which must include both the previous positions. It must, in other words, be able to understand and accept man as a replaceable individual, and at the same time to preserve his irreplaceability. The concept of representation appears suited to achieve this mediation, because, far from obliterating man's irreplaceability, it actually requires and safeguards it. The synthesis of assertion and counter-assertion, of thesis and antithesis, therefore reads: the individual man is irreplaceable *yet* representable.

6

THE STRUCTURE OF REPRESENTATION

WE ASSUME HERE that in no sense does man 'stand for himself and himself alone'. This heroic conception of irreplaceability cannot survive the test of reality. The decisive moments in life are not those which call for the heroics of 'no help to him there by another is shown'. On the contrary, the individual knows he is dependent and need not be ashamed of this. He can accept himself as one who knows his own weakness yet does not despair of it. He does not pretend to be anything better or more complete. He neither idealizes himself as self-sufficient and irreplaceable, nor goes to the other extreme of an exchangeability so complete that even the question of personal identity does not arise. By accepting himself in his weakness and dependence, he continues, consciously or unconsciously, his search for a representative. But are there not in fact situations in which the individual really does depend on himself alone? Are there not areas of experience where there is neither dependence nor representation? Such situations undoubtedly exist, the only question is *where*—in what kind of life situation? It is not for nothing that Schiller sings the praises of the 'conflict' in which a man 'still counts for something', for there is no representation in that primordial non-neutral area of experience where a man must prove himself in direct face-to-face encounter. We can start here from one of two different basic patterns of human life, as Hegel has presented them in the dialectic of 'master' and 'slave',[1] the conflict pattern and the work pattern. When life is interpreted in terms of the conflict pattern, the relationship to

---

[1] *Phänomenologie des Geistes*, ed. Hoffmeister, p. 146ff; ET Baillie, pp. 177ff.

the other person will be experienced as immediate: as sub-
mission, enforced recognition, hate or love, enmity or community. The neutrality of things, of the 'it', has not yet inter-
vened weakeningly between the 'I' and its desire. The 'I' and
the 'thou' confront one another directly, without mediation,
as friend or foe. But even for Schiller this conflict pattern was
already a historical memory, something which continued to
apply even though now in the world of work—the world of the
normal situation in contrast to the abnormal situation of conflict—one man can in fact answer for another and representation is possible.

For here already the conflict pattern has been superseded by
the more complex and modern, if far less studied, work pattern:
meaning, by work, production on the principle of the division
of labour. The relationship to the other man has been mediated
into the world and become roundabout and indirect. On the
way to the 'thou', the 'I' takes a detour, via things, through the
'it'. But in the course of this detour it is at the same time restored to itself, related back to itself in a new and more refracted
way. In the work pattern, *ratio* triumphs over life, renunciation
over desire, mediation over immediacy, replaceability over
irreplaceability. This process of neutralization also involves for
man a different way of thinking about himself, one which is
quite impossible within the conflict pattern. What might be
discounted as an occasional failure due to sickness, immaturity
or weakness, so long as the 'I' was not an object of reflection,
becomes constitutive once man begins this more inclusive reflection upon himself, which historically speaking was developed
by the Christian faith. The experiences a man has of himself
within the horizon of this process of reflection are not exactly
encouraging. Considering what is expected of him in the new
work pattern—in the way of courage, energy, and readiness to
believe, hope, and love, for example—the self-sufficiency of the
individual becomes less and less credible, the higher the level of
reflection he reaches. Not surprisingly, the heroic epoch, the age
of the hero who 'stands for himself and himself alone', always

occurs at the beginning of recognizable historical periods, when man's discouraging experiences of himself still lie ahead. When life is seen in terms of the conflict pattern, when man's relation to the other person seems to be immediate and unrefracted, these experiences—resignation where there should be hope, indifference instead of love, scepticism instead of faith—still await man's discovery. It requires a certain naivety to be able to regard oneself as self-sufficient and independent. But when work supersedes universal conflict, man's self-sufficiency is increasingly abandoned.

The conflict pattern is represented as excluding any division of labour. Self-sufficiency is glorified. The warrior is not replaceable. In conflict he achieves his identity. The worker, by contrast, buries his identity; someone else could always do what he does. Heroic self-sufficiency is now replaced by dependence and responsibility, each requiring the other. The worker is not sure of his identity. He goes on seeking it and, in this longing to realize his identity, dependence appears as an anthropological structure. Because personal being—except in conflict—means dependent being, man needs to be represented.

The phenomenon of dependence has been described from the most varied anthropological standpoints. Dependence is expressed biologically in the extreme helplessness and exceptionally prolonged childhood and puberty of the human child compared with young animals. Man's dependence is equally evident when work is regarded as the basic anthropological factor, as it is by Hegel and Marx. Man and beast are here differentiated by the manner in which they obtain their food. Human life is already social in structure in this respect.

The production of life, both of one's own by labour and of fresh life by procreation, appears at once as a double relationship, on the one hand as a natural, on the other as a social relationship. By social is meant the co-operation of several individuals, no matter under what conditions, in what manner or to what end.[1]

[1] Karl Marx, *Frühschriften*, Stuttgart, 1953, p. 356. ET in T. B. Bottomore and M. Rubel, *Karl Marx, Selected Writings in Sociology and Social Philosophy*, London, 1956, p. 62.

This social relationship implies dependent existence and demands representation by the very fact that it is necessarily social. This dependence on representation is present as an everyday experience wherever men live together and whatever the form of society. It relates not just to an individual 'thou' who takes responsibility for another, but equally to a socially mediated 'thou' which has been formed into groups, established itself in human affairs and embodied itself in institutions. Our dependence is therefore dependence upon society, which is able to represent us not only individually and personally but also collectively and multiformly.

The question remains, however, whether this representation —offered and given by society—is adequate, and whether much that is irreparable does not remain, requiring representation of a kind which society is not yet in a position to provide. Defective planning, mistakes and failures in production, could be irrevocable and destructive of life were it not that work, as a social phenomenon, ensured exchange, substitution, and even representation. But who is to make good the deficiencies which do not result from work alone nor are to be made good by work alone?

The representation which society does afford the individual certainly provides concrete patterns for the structure of representation. But these structure patterns remain empty if they cannot be applied outside the social relationship. (We are dependent and need representation even when no one can represent us—when we die, for example.) By 'outside' we do not mean a place where man could, so to speak, be relieved of his social being; rather a situation where it is no longer possible to appeal to already existent phenomena. No further purpose would be served here by an analysis of this situation, even though it could throw light on the forms which dependence takes.

As something we inquire into, dependence reaches out beyond the representation provided by society. Whether this inquiry is answered and its expectation fulfilled, or, as can happen, dependence is—simply and without frustration—accepted as a fact, is primarily a theological problem.

In the present context, where we inquire into the structure of representation, there is another essential aspect of the irreplaceable individual, namely, his dependent being as a radical expression of his being-in-time. Only someone who needs time can be dependent, just as only someone who has time can be represented. Anyone who has run out of time is replaced. The irreplaceable man who imagines he cannot even be represented is also a man without time, estranged from the perspective of temporality, and in this respect comparable to a replaceable thing. For, in the search for personal identity, time is not merely an annoying shackle, a freak finite condition, but actually the hope of those who lack identity. If I am irreplaceable but can be represented, I have gained time. Moreover, this means that I am as a person irreplaceable only in an incomplete form, which is far removed from the depersonalized idea of substitution. For it is the very people who regard me as irreplaceable who take my helplessness, my immaturity, my temporary incapacity into account. It is precisely those who regard me as irreplaceable who are grieved by my absence, my silence, my illness, my death. The idea of representation actually acquires its basis in the very place where the individual's irreplaceability is maintained. Indeed, all the conditions which make representation necessary appear only where irreplaceability is presupposed. Where I am irreplaceable, I must be represented; because I am irreplaceable, I must be represented.

We have, with that, defined the conditions under which representation can appear: personality and temporality. If the person is no longer regarded as irreplaceable, representation becomes unnecessary, substitution will do. Only the irreplaceable man, who cannot abandon the search for personal identity, wants to be represented; but for him it is essential. He depends upon representation because he exists in time. His temporality necessarily includes both dependence and responsibility, each corresponding to the other. Whenever man is not thought of as a person existing in time, that is to say, whenever he is thought of either as timeless and self-sufficient or as non-personal and therefore replaceable, the necessary conditions of representation are missing.

Particular forms of representation, based on personality and temporality, are dependence and responsibility—according to whether the standpoint is that of the one represented or that of the representative. We experience representation when we are dependent on another or on others, and when we bear responsibility for another or for others. The two aspects belong inseparably together. The moment either aspect is divorced from its dialectical correlate, both personality and temporality are in danger. An absolutized dependence can at any time involve the reduction of the person to immaturity, while a responsibility which has become exclusive can become an undisguised tyranny, exercised by some over others. A dependence which is not prepared in certain circumstances to accept responsibility slips back into an immaturity which is no longer temporary. It becomes fixed in childishness, slides into total dependence. Anyone who wants 'redemption' without exercising responsibility, anyone who wants only to be represented but not to exist representatively himself, will at some point also be ready to pay the far too high price of renouncing responsible action altogether and of abandoning the world to itself.

It is just as easy to think of responsibility without dependence. When that happens, those who take responsibility often become, contrary to their express intention, tyrants who have forgotten that representation is always temporary and conditional, and only in this way personal.

PART TWO

BETWEEN MAGIC AND SUBSTITUTION
Representation in the History of Theology

'In the field of finitude, the characteristic idea is
that each remains what he is. If he has done evil, he
is evil; evil is in him as his quality. But in the sphere
of morality, still more in that of religion, Spirit is
already known to be free, to be affirmative in itself
... Spirit can make what has happened as if it had
not happened.'[1]

[1] Hegel, *Philosophie der Religion*, ed. Lasson, Vol. XIV, pp. 172f. ET by E. B.
Speirs and J. Sanderson, *Lectures on the Philosophy of Religion*, London, 1895, Vol. 3,
p. 96.

7

INTRODUCTION

WHO AM I? 'The freedom of the subject . . . to have infinite value and also to become aware of this ultimacy'—we can take this as agreed, with Hegel. Agreed, at least, as the 'goal' of the Spirit, who wills identity and cannot abandon identity except at the cost of renouncing itself. But this being which has infinite value and is irreplaceable, must be represented. He needs representation because he is dependent, as the various anthropological findings show. To this dependence corresponds the capacity to assume responsibility. But the representation needed and exercised is not just a postulate of the practical reason; it is something 'which happens' 'again and again in human life in a thousand varying degrees, if very seldom in the extreme form I have indicated'.[1] Because men depend on representation wherever they live in society, representation is itself a universal phenomenon. In the Christian faith, the reality of representation is brought to self-awareness. Identity here appears in the figure of the Representative, and not in an unmediated, unrefracted form. The man who seeks identity experiences it as representation, needed and exercised in the form of responsibility and dependence. Within the horizon of this experience he has come up against the temporality of existence as never before. The consciousness of finitude is uniquely, more sharply defined in the Christian faith than in any comparable religion. That we need time before we die, and indeed filled, qualified time—time for identity to appear in non-identity—is a Christian idea which

[1] F. Gogarten, *Was ist Christentum?* Göttingen, 1956, p. 27.

finds radical expression in dependence on the Representative.

The Christian faith radicalized the idea of representation in an unprecedented way: it made representation the effective and potent basic event of existence. It elevated the Representative as the decisive figure of world history who bears all things—namely, the sin of the world. It removed the temporal and local limitations of the representation he carried out, and thus made it universal.

But this radicalizing was only possible, and only succeeded, where the Christian faith was freed from the toils of magical ideas. It was certainly no accident that in our search for a pattern of representation our attention lighted on the fairy tale and was drawn to the world of magic. In the non-magic world since the Enlightenment, the idea of representation has increasingly lost ground. Outside theological circles, the 'office of representation' is regarded by many as a technical term in dogmatics and rejected as such. Little attempt has been made to disentangle its meaning from its magical associations. The term 'representation' may still retain its meaning in law, sociology, and psychology, but in theology it has become colourless. It is in danger of migrating from systematic theology to the science of religion where it still has domiciliary rights.[1]

Still more unfortunate than this virtual withdrawal of a basic concept, or rather its emigration, is the naive way it is sometimes used; for such usage, however natural it may seem, inevitably conjures up magical ideas. Representation is simply assumed and the question how the principle of representation can apply at all (or is even conceivable in an enlightened world where each individual must answer for himself) is not even raised. For example, in his book on the primitive Christian idea of time and history, Oscar Cullmann uses the 'principle of re-

[1] For example, the first edition of *Religion in Geschichte und Gegenwart*, 1907, mentions 'representation' only in its church law connotation of 'deputizing' for pastors. The second and third editions of 1927 and 1963 illustrate the concept of 'representation' with material drawn from the history of religion, citing as an example the reference to the scapegoat in Leviticus 16. A reference to Christ's representation, included by Bertholet in the second edition, is absent from the third.

presentation' as a key concept without ever once discussing it but simply taking it on trust, that is to say, reading it off historically and exegetically. The result is that the event of representation itself remains formal and empty. Representative election is formulated in terms of a pre-personal mode of thought and presented as a 'progressive reduction'—from humanity to the people of Israel, from Israel to the 'remnant' and so on, down to the incarnate Christ. *How far* the history of a single people can in any sense be decisive for the salvation of all peoples we are not told. This neat pattern of a saving history which then progresses from the apostles, the Church, the remnant and the 'people of the saints', down to redeemed humanity in the kingdom of God,[1] is based on a concept of representation which allows any personalist view of the matter to be abandoned: a magical conception which clearly resembles the technological view of representation as substitution, which will concern us later. Wolfhart Pannenberg, whose view of representation frequently approaches the one taken here, has a different conception of the 'universal horizon of representation'.[2] He removes the concept out of range of the criticism levelled against it by the enlightenment, particularly as developed by the Socinians. Pannenberg develops his view of representation with the help of principles underlying the Jewish view and concept of sin and expiation. That is to say, his 'provisional interpretation' is not formed by phenomena like exchange and irreplaceability, but primarily by tradition. Guided by this, he seeks to harmonize the 'accidental historical facts' of Israel's tradition with the 'necessary truths' of modern anthropology. His starting points are, first, the 'natural connection between deed and consequence'; and second, and inseparable from this, 'the involvement of the individual in society'. These two complexes are thought of in sufficiently general terms to make translation from the world of the past appear possible. Even so, the Enlightenment's criticism of the notion of a mythical exchange of

---

[1] O. Cullmann, *Christ and Time*, London, 1949, pp. 116f.
[2] W. Pannenberg, *Grundzüge der Christologie*, Gütersloh, 1964, pp. 271ff.

deeds and their consequences is still not being taken with sufficient seriousness, as long as the irreplaceable character of the individual is not seen as the basis of all criticism of a magical, mythical view of representation. The modern threat to the notion of the irreplaceable individual hardly seems to be taken into account, for Pannenberg finds it possible to collectivize him by the use of Old Testament conceptions of social history. The criticism Pannenberg legitimately levels at individualism fails to solve the problem of subjectivity with its unrelinquishable question about personal identity. Clearly, despite these new attempts, contemporary Protestant theology in general has lost a definite possibility of thinking and speaking which was still available to theology in an earlier period. One is dealing here with an incomprehensible factor, and because only substitution, not representation, can be exercised in a depersonalized world, even well intentioned talk of representation like Pannenberg's cannot help obstructing the view. Only in the course of our inquiry will the extent to which traditional theology nevertheless succeeded in developing a personalist view of representation emerge; also how far it preserved or even understood the irreplaceable individual in its view of representation. At all events, a critical touchstone exists by which to assess traditional theology. It is the question, how far did such theology interpret representation in personal terms?

8

THE MAGICAL INTERPRETATION

A MAGICAL VIEW of representation is a typical phenomenon of religion. We find traces of it in almost all religions. The Egyptians, for example, placed little models of wood, stone, or clay in the tombs of their dead. These models were known as *ushabti*, 'answerers' or 'helpers'. The abode of the dead was thought of as simply a continuation of this world. Within it was a broad open land called *Earu*, through whose fertile fields flowed another Nile. In this land work in plenty awaited the dead. If the dead man was assigned too hard or menial a task, he could, by using magical formulas, arrange for the 'answerer' or 'helper' to do it for him. 'When I am ordered to irrigate the river banks, then shalt thou say: Here am I!'[1] What exactly happens here? Underlying this Egyptian belief in the power of the *ushabti* to help the dead is the idea that every living thing is magically identified with its image. What happens to a man's image happens to the man himself. What the image does benefits the man. The *ushabti* really do represent the dead man. When they work, he is left in peace. They perform the duties assigned to him. Since Frazer, such actions are generally described as 'imitative magic'.[2] The answerers imitate the dead man. Acting for him, they relieve him from the necessity to act himself. There are a number of reasons why the relations between the dead man and his wooden slaves may be termed 'magical'. For

[1] F. Bertholet, *Wörterbuch der Religionen*, ed. H. V. Campenhausen, Kröner 1952, S.V. 'Stellevertretung' and 'Ushebti'. See too, A. H. Sayce, *The Religion of Ancient Egypt*, pp. 51ff.
[2] Sigmund Freud, *The Standard Edition of the Complete Psychological Works*, ed. James Strachey, Vol. XIII, *Totem and Tabu and other works*, London 1955, p. 81.

one thing, the represener is a thing and not a person. The
request for representation is sure to be met; the 'answerer' is
merely a function of the dead man. Connected with this is the
fact that representation is here the normal usage which need
only be correctly followed for everything to happen as desired;
it is never something unexpected or miraculous. The one making the request runs no risk of being denied it. Finally, the representation exercised here lacks the essential note of the temporary and transient, despite the fact that it is incomplete and
relates only to a specific task. The *ushabti* do not represent 'for
the time being' only, or with a view to their own displacement.

For our present purpose, we find here an astonishing parallel
between this sort of representation taken from the realm of
imitative magic and the concept of substitution, already briefly
touched on. Neither is intrinsically personal nor time-condi-
tioned. In both, replacement is complete and permanent.

Even the Old Testament, which elsewhere de-magicized and
de-mythicized so many elements common to all religious history,
does not rise above this level, if we leave out of account the
approaches to personal representation in Jeremiah, Hosea, and
Second Isaiah. For example, the concept of the scapegoat[1] does
not go beyond the circle of imitative magic. Sin is presented as
something physical. The priest identifies the sin of the people
with the goat by laying his hands on its head and confessing
over it all the sins of the people. The goat, a domestic animal
and as such belonging to and closely associated with man,
suffers in place of man. Instead of the sinful people, who deserve
the punishment, it is the goat which is driven into the desert,
into the desolate, unclean, unholy place. The sin can no longer
defile the people. The original role of the scapegoat, then, is
focused on its being driven away[2]; the idea of representative
punishment is foreign to the passage, as is that of sacrifice, which
cannot be introduced here. No importance whatever is attached
to the special condition of the goat—to its being unblemished
and perfect, for example—for the simple reason that the idea of

[1] Lev. 16.   [2] Lev. 16.22.

sacrifice played no part at all in the earlier history of such representative purification rites.

The important thing is not *who* removes the sin. What matters is that it disappears from the human sphere. In other religions, the remover can be a human being, another kind of animal, or very often some object, a stick or stone, which can be loaded with the sin and slung away. The Babylonian priest would say: 'Let the evil be torn from me, and let the bird carry it away into the heavens.'[1] Frequently a vehicle is used as a scapegoat. The Biajas of Borneo annually sent a little boat out to sea laden with the sins and misfortunes of the people. Anyone coming into contact with the boat was infected with evil.[2] Here too, sin is thought of as physical impurity. Representation is accordingly understood in magical terms as a transfer and removal.

We find here an essential affinity between magic and technology: between the practice of magical representation and transfer, on the one hand, and technological replaceability and exchangeability, on the other. Once again the elements of personality and temporality, which we have shown to be essential to representation when regarded as a personal transaction, are missing. Magic and technology can work only in terms of substitution, based as they are on universal interchangeability. This affinity should not be used by the theologians to nourish hopes of understanding the structures of magic or to regard these structures as a point of contact. For while interchangeability is certainly common to both magical representation and technological substitution, the explanation of it is not the same in the two cases. In magical thinking, no distinction has yet been made between things and persons; in other words, such a distinction can always be ignored. Things, plants, animals and man exist in an original solidarity which permits their interchangeability in certain conditions, such as time, place, or magical formula. And this original solidarity of all things is intimately related to the uncontrollability of all things.

[1] M. Jastrow, *Die Religion Babyloniens und Assyriens*, 1912, Vol. II, p. 95.
[2] Frazer, *The Golden Bough, A Study in Magic and Religion*, 3rd ed. 1913, Part IV, 'The Scapegoat', p. 200.

When everything is uncontrollable, when mystery lies on all sides, when literally 'nothing can be made of it' all, one thing can always answer for another. Even the injury or pain inflicted on one person can be experienced in the body of another. And what makes this alienation, this exchange, possible is just this total uncontrollability. In other words, the individual's helplessness finds its correlate in what Freud called the omnipotence of thoughts,[1] which makes exchange possible.

This ceaseless exchange is not limited even by sin and death. The omnipotence of thoughts involves the removal of temporal, spatial, and objective natural limitations. What is remote in space and separated in time can easily be brought together by an act of the consciousness. This is the only kind of removal of limitations open to helplessness. A removal of limitations has also taken place in technological thinking, through the complete replaceability of all things. Here the interchangeability of things and persons depends on the possibility of producing them. When the world is conceived in terms of complete controllability, everything can be replaced by something else. Things become 'wares', everything is the product of human labour. Each particular product can be exchanged for another. The complete exchangeability once achieved by magic is now achieved by technology. Mediation is omnipotence now; the omnipotence not of thoughts but of manufacture. Magical representation, a natural growth on the soil of a pre-personal era, approximates to the technological substitution of post-personal thought.

[1] Sigmund Freud, *The Standard Edition*, ed. J. Strachey, Vol. XIII, p. 85.

9

REPRESENTATION IN THE NEW TESTAMENT

WE SHOULD NOT attach undue importance to the fact that the term 'representative' does not appear in the New Testament. The thing itself is there, and the recurring phrase ὑπὲρ ἡμῶν, used to express it, probably belongs to the oldest stratum of the tradition which Paul found already in existence. Paul himself exploys a whole series of metaphors derived from concepts already formulated, in order to express the significance of Christ's sufferings and death. From the Jewish conception of worship came the idea of expiatory sacrifice with its juristic flavour, as well as the idea of the atoning medium—transferred by Paul to the blood of Jesus—and the idea of the representative cultic sacrifice. From Gnostic mythology came the idea of the *redeemed Redeemer* who constitutes one 'body' with those who belong to him and whose experiences, such as death and resurrection, also happen to those who belong to his 'body'.[1] None of these various and divergent images being adequate to express the saving event, they were adopted and then set aside. They were not hardened into a technical terminology, though the apostle was quite capable of doing this in other connections. They circle around the reality we are seeking to indicate by the term 'representation', from various angles, and without the concept ever becoming explicit. Yet implicitly they radicalize the concept by liberating it from the magical view of representation.

[1] Rudolf Bultmann, *Theology of the New Testament*, 1952, Vol. I, chapter 3, section 15, 'Gnostic Motifs'.

This liberation was effected by the following elements which became distinctive of the Christian view: historicity, universalization, voluntariness, and suffering. Representation was first radically conceived when it was inseparably attached to a definite person accessible to *historical knowledge*. The situation is not that everyone and everything can represent every other— not even a group of the finest magicians or a collection of the objects touched by them—but rather that one particular man achieves representation in a definite geographical situation, in definite fixed and investigable historical conditions. The historicity of the Representative points to his uncontrollability, his freedom. For magical thinking *some* representative is always available; if not this one then another. But in the Christian view, there is representation *only* in this name. The action and suffering of this particular historical person fulfilled in advance all subsequent as well as all previous, all actual and all potential action and suffering by other persons.

There is therefore, matching the historical concentration right down to the crib at Bethlehem, a universalization into the 'once and for all', crossing the barriers of space and time. Whereas in magical thinking a different representative is needed for each different situation, the Christian Representative acted once and for all. With the exclusion of all notions of magical efficacy, all confinement within communal notions likewise disappears. In contrast to the earlier conception, in which the scapegoat represents the people who have sinned and deserve punishment, there is here both a concentration and a widening of the reality of representation. Since it no longer works like magic, representation does not apply blanket-fashion to particular groups as such: it is not necessary to belong already to a certain group in order to be saved. On the contrary, it creates its own new collectives or groups which are inherently open-ended. Individuation and universalization go hand in hand. Because membership of a particular national group is no longer decisive, any more than membership of a particular race, class or section of society, representation can now become effective for the world, for every world. The new concept of the Representative is both particular and universal, each of these aspects conditioning the other.

This universalization, following the historical concentration, can obviously lead back once more into the error of magical thinking. The thought of the One who made satisfaction for all tempts us to overlook the fact that the Representative only represents us 'for the time being', only incompletely and conditionally. The very removal of the limits to representation can mislead us into thinking in terms of magical substitution, with the result that the irreplaceability of the represented, instead of being safeguarded by Christ's representation, can be sacrificed in the interests of a universal history of salvation. The inseparability of historicity and the removal of limits, of individuation and universalization, reminds us once more of the relationship 'irreplaceable yet representable' in which the individual is dependent on a form of representation which has made temporality its inalienable criterion. Christology and anthropology correspond. This tension between 'irreplaceable' and 'representable', between unconditionality and detachability, between personality as non-interchangeability and the role as constant replaceability, is indicated in the New Testament by the preposition ὑπέρ, the preposition of representation.[1] As the antitype of Adam, Christ is the summing up of humanity,[2] and is therefore our Representative before God. Because his person is representative, his action and suffering are representative too, applying to all those he represents, in other words, to all men.[3] The Representative assumes the destiny of those he represents, the destiny of dying after meaningless life.[4] He dies 'for' them, that is to say in their place. The 'just' dies 'for' the unjust.[5]

With that, the third characteristic of the Christian idea of

---

[1] See W. F. Arndt and F. W. Gingrich, *A Greek-English Lexicon of the NT*, 1957, where, under ὑπέρ c.gen., are given the meanings: 'for', 'in behalf of', 'for the sake of' someone. When used in the sense of representation, ὑπέρ is associated with verbs like 'request, pray, care, work, feel, suffer, die, support'.

[2] Rom. 5.   [3] II Cor. 5.15.   [4] Rom. 5.6.   [5] I Pet. 3.18.

representation comes into view: namely, voluntariness, as a further structural element of personal representation. The representation known and described in the New Testament can be characterized as 'personal' because it does not rest on a magical universal solidarity but on an act of association that is personal and voluntary. It rests not on identity but on an act of identification, not on a previous being but on an actual event. Christ took our place voluntarily and not under some physical compulsion of his 'divine nature'. Nor is his act of reconciliation to be regarded as completed all at once, as something objectifiable in the past. If Christ's representation were simply a particular deed, previously agreed with God, then Christ merely plays the role usually associated with the whipping boy. It is a vital element in Christ's existence as a person that his representation should be an unfinished and continuing relationship, and not something he exercises all at once by virtue of a distinctive supernatural quality.

This leads on naturally to the fourth new element in the distinctive Christian view of representation, namely, the suffering of the Representative. Judaism at the time of Jesus did not expect a suffering Messiah. This is plain both from the attitude of Jesus' opponents[1] and his disciples.[2] Jesus reinterpreted the concept 'Son of man' in such a way that the title now expressed the insignificance and helplessness of the one who suffers for others. Jewish exegesis had applied the figure of the suffering servant of God in Isaiah 53 to the people of Israel, while later Judaism explicitly rejected the idea of a suffering Messiah. The Targum on the Isaiah passage eliminates that which concerns the suffering of the servant. The idea that one individual should by his suffering and death act representatively for the whole world was quite unique. This is also shown by the parallel Qumran texts referring to the suffering of the 'Teacher of Righteousness'. Even this is not voluntarily accepted representative suffering.[3] The despised Messiah of the Christians, however,

[1] John 12.34.
[2] Matt. 16.22; Luke 18.34 and 24.21.
[3] 'Christologie' in *Religion in Geschichte und Gegenwart*, 3, 1963.

proves himself to be God's elect precisely by his suffering.

Glancing back at the magical interpretation, we may compare the request of the dead Egyptian seeking the help of his 'answerer' with the prayer of the Christian in Paul Gerhardt's hymn 'O Haupt voll Blut und Wunden.' The former says: 'When I am ordered to irrigate the river banks, then shalt thou say, Here am I!' But the Christian hymn says: 'When sorest fears overwhelm my heart, tear me from them by thy fear and pain.' The fear, the helplessness, the dependence on another, are comparable. The sole difference lies in the Christian's plea —'by thy fear and pain'. But this contains all the elements of representation just described: universalization, historicity, voluntariness, suffering. To this dying God anyone can turn. He bears a definite, historically recognizable face. Voluntarily he made himself the representative to whom appeal is made here. He did so through suffering. The basis which makes this representation possible is its indissoluble connection with a particular historical person.

10

THE JURISTIC INTERPRETATION

THESE CHARACTERISTICS OF representation are inalienable. They have sufficed to prevent the unchallenged domination of Christian theology by a magical understanding of representation, but they cannot themselves ensure a personalist interpretation. It is always possible to employ juristic concepts to explain Christ's representation and so very appreciably to reduce the personal being of the men represented in the interests of the divine being of God.

The juristic approach to an understanding of representation has had the greatest influence in theology in the form of Anselm's satisfaction theory. Anselm's basic idea is that God's honour has sustained injury by reason of man's sin. On this view, God's relation to men is not simply private and personal but that of a ruler, of a king who governs a state. It would therefore not be enough for God simply to show mercy, simply to cancel sin. That would be to destroy order in God's kingdom. As *lèse-majesté*, sin has robbed God of something of his honour, and this must be restored. God's righteousness necessarily requires one of two things: *aut poena aut satisfactio*. Since it is not God's will to destroy men, which would be the only appropriate penalty, only the way of *satisfactio* remains. But men cannot provide this *satisfactio* since their sin, as *lèse-majesté*, is infinitely great and the *satisfactio* itself must therefore be more than the sum total of the world. It is therefore impossible 'unless there be someone who can pay God for the sin of man somewhat greater than all which is not God'.[1] Only Christ can really

[1] Anselm, *Cur Deus Homo?* Migne, P.L. 158, c. 403; ET Richard Church, Edinburgh 1909, p. 66.

'satisfy' God in our place. Only the God-man by his voluntary death performs an equivalent act whose value as an offering is proportionate to the value of his life. He alone can perform an act of infinite value which is at the same time a human act. Christ's representation consists therefore in the making of this *satisfactio* and not, for example, in suffering in our stead.[1]

In the context of our search for a personalist conception of representation, Anselm's personalist view of sin is important. He regards sin not just as a lapse in some particular respect or other, but as an affront to God, *exhonoratio Dei*. The disorder of the world which God cannot possibly ignore is the direct consequence of this dishonouring of God. Because of the seriousness and weight of this sin, forgiveness can never mean indulgence. Yet it is precisely when we reflect on the root of this profound idea that we encounter the greatest difficulty: the problem presented by the acceptance of a satisfaction made by another. Why does God accept this, why is he satisfied by it, unless there is already something prior to the act of satisfaction which inclines him to the authentic act of forgiveness? In other words, is *satisfactio* as an objectifiable fact sufficient to explain forgiveness as a voluntary act? What view of God lies behind all this? The notion that 'in himself' God is irreconcilable and needs first to be appeased by Christ's act, finds no support in the New Testament, least of all in Paul. There, God is certainly not reconciled by something outside himself. On the contrary, it is he who 'reconciles the world unto himself'.[2] In the act of reconciliation, God is the subject, the agent. In Anselm's presentation, Christ stands facing God, so to speak, but with his back to us. God is reconciled by what Christ 'restores' to him, and can therefore now have a new relationship to us. How far this Christ enables us to acquire a new being, is not considered. While it is true, and indeed the basis of Anselm's greatness, that this theory excluded all human attempts at self-redemption, all idea of righteousness through works, all reduction of religion to mere

[1] For a critique of Anselm, see W. Koehler, *Dogmengeschichte* [2]1943, p. 304.
[2] II Cor. 5, 19.

73

moralism, it is also true that the relation of God and man is here progressively legalized. This is due to the use of categories which possibly originated in Germanic notions of honour and loyalty, and which, while retaining a core open to interpretation in personal terms, in time produced unfortunate consequences. For one thing, the theory limited God's freedom, for it makes him the object and no longer the subject of the act of reconciliation. Again, it is only indirectly that Christ acts 'for us', his representation being narrowly circumscribed and in fact confined legalistically to one particular unrepeatable action. The representative intervenes for those represented, not with his whole existence, but with one particular act. Further, because the emphasis is on what is done in representation, representation is inevitably interpreted in exclusive terms, and its provisional character is missing. Christ stands where we shall never stand, either actually or potentially; his action creates salvation independently of those he represents.

Once theology began to root its thinking more strongly in God's reconciliation with man, it would abandon the methodological alternative *aut poena aut satisfactio*, which for Anselm was fundamental. A clear illustration of this is Luther's Christology. He used the term *satisfactio* with reserve. In his view it was too restricted and he would have preferred to leave it to the lawyers.[1] But when he does use it, he does so not in the Anselmian sense of something which happens primarily in relation to God and is intended to make reconciliation possible for God. For Luther, *satisfactio* is the fulfilment of the law and therefore directed from the outset towards men. Christ fulfils the law and bears the penalty of sin and the divine wrath, not 'in order to reconcile God but rather in order to break the power of sin, wrath, and law, by which men are kept apart from God'.[2] The concept of the *meritum Christi* now appears, not with reference to God, but as part of Luther's polemic against human merit. It was with reference to men that Christ made satisfac-

[1] Luther, *Werke, Kritische Gesamtausgabe*, ed. Knaake, Weimar 1883ff, Vol. 34, I, p. 303.
[2] F. Gogarten, *Die Verkündigung Jesu Christi*, 1948, p. 358.

tion. But his action does not alter God and his attitude to us— God's absolute righteousness. Instead of making reparation, Christ suffers God's punishment and wrath. The very thing which is missing in Anselm's treatment, namely Christ's relationship to us, is made central in Luther. Christ satisfies and liberates our inmost conscience by regarding God's wrath as just, deserved, necessary, and therefore itself merciful.[1]

The basic problem of representation, which Anselm took to be the problem of *satisfactio*, presented itself to Luther in quite a different way and in his reflection upon it he made use of another term, *imputatio*, which he borrowed from Ockham. The problem of imputation was generally taken to be how far a particular sin or merit could morally or even legally be 'imputed' to its responsible agent.[2]

In the strictly theological sense, imputation is the act whereby God 'attributes' or imputes to the sinner the righteousness of Christ and does not 'attribute' or impute to the sinner his own sin. Since in Luther the function of the concept *imputatio* is analogous to that of *satisfactio* in Anselm, attention is directed away from the God (whose kingdom has been thrown into disorder by man's treason or *lèse-majesté* and who needs to be reconciled) and towards the man who can only acquire righteousness by way of twofold imputation, the non-imputation of sin and the *imputatio meriti Christi*.

Contrary to my deserts and my worth, God attributes to me the active and passive obedience of Christ. But the forensic character of this justification is extremely questionable, for the conscience rebels against this proposed balancing of the books.

Sin just is not a failure in performance which might be balanced by the positive performance of 'another'. As a performance the *meritum* could only balance an objectifiable failure in performance. If on the contrary sin is my *own* lapse, if it must be thought of as necessarily a lapse of the person, it cannot be made good by a balancing performance introduced into the reckoning in my favour.[3]

---

[1] Luther, *Werke*, W. A. Vol. 40, II, p. 3.
[2] Cf. 'Rechtfertigung' in *Religion in Geschichte und Gegenwart*, 1963.
[3] Otto Weber, *Grundlagen der Dogmatik*, Vol. II, 1962, p. 346.

This criticism certainly applies to Luther if we take him literally, just as it applies to his quite inadequate conceptual framework. But materially, Luther's purpose is not to make the balancing performance the basis of theological imputation. The basis of theological imputation is that in Christ God's relationship to man has changed and can now be known to be changed.

In morality and law, imputation is merely declaratory; it reacts to a given state of affairs but creates nothing new. God's imputation by contrast is the creative word which calls into being that which does not exist; it presents to the unjust man to whom it imputes righteousness the possibility of being righteous and does so by this very act of declaring him righteous.[1]

God regards man as righteous. This is not to be taken as pretence on God's part, engaged in by him as an academic exercise, and leaving the actual existence of the sinner unredeemed. Certain expressions of Luther certainly come close to suggesting such a pretence, as emerges clearly in Melanchthon's exegesis of Luther, for example, the phrase *peccator in re, iustus in spe*, which suggests that the substance of the person—his nature as sinner—remains unchanged in justification. And indeed, Luther is concerned to show that it is not the nature of the person which is justified—for all such thinking mistakenly regards righteousness as a possession, whereas for Luther righteousness must always remain 'alien', that is to say, a gift. The theory of imputation safeguards the truth that man never 'has' righteousness in the sense of some objectifiable possession which once acquired becomes inalienable. Its basis, assumed but never explicit in Luther, is a different anthropology from that which begins from man's 'nature'. God regards the person not in terms of substance but in terms of relationship. The theory of imputation is concerned with the relationship—expressed juristically but intended existentially—of man to God. This relationship, the theory asserts, is the only basis of existence. God regards man as if he were righteous. This 'as if' is not contrasted

[1] See article 'Imputatio' in *Religion in Geschichte und Gegenwart*.

76

with some supposedly known or measurable reality but, on the contrary, creates the reality. There are not two levels: one of man's being and nature; the other, man as seen by God. For God, only one thing counts, namely, how he regards a man. According to the theory of imputation, man is so completely in God's hands that what counts is not what he 'is' or 'has' but only what he is 'regarded' as being.

God does not impute righteousness like a teacher employing a pedagogical trick—his opinion of man hurrying on ahead of man's real being, confident that this 'as if' pattern will in the end produce real righteousness. The fact is rather that, as Luther sees it, God's ontology is different, being based not on substances but on relationship. God believes in man. In a new relationship, freely established by God *sola gratia*, man not only can be but really is new. Imputed righteousness (the 'trick') cannot therefore be anything else but effective righteousness. The new relationship *is* the new being. No different, no more secure, no more substantial being is envisaged.

Using the concept of imputed righteousness, Luther expressed an understanding of the person which makes the reckoning of performances in the satisfaction theory quite unimportant in comparison. Christ's assumption of sin[1] is the application of this complete relation-izing of the person. Christ regarded himself as existing purely on the basis of dependence. He regarded himself purely in the way God regarded him. What he is or has, his sinlessness or his blessedness, is nothing to him. How God deals with him is everything. This utter surrender to God's verdict forms the foundation of the representation which Christ performs for us. Christ does for us what we are incapable of doing. He surrenders himself to God. He does this provisionally in order that we may be able to do it too.

---

[1] 'I did the sin which Martin did'—Luther, *Werke* W. A. Vol. 40, I, p. 442.

I I

HEGEL'S ANSWER
TO MORAL IMPUTATION

LUTHER'S PERSONALIST APPROACH was very imperfectly preserved in Lutheran orthodoxy. The Enthusiasts and Anabaptists failed to grasp what Luther meant by imputed righteousness, fearing it would inevitably lead to moral laxity or, in theological language, 'cheap grace'. Nor was it understood by those who, like Melanchthon, stressed the forensic character of imputation as a divine verdict pronounced and in force in heaven. The unity of imputed and effective righteousness, which Luther at least sought to safeguard, broke up. While orthodox Lutheranism put all the emphasis on imputation, interpreting it lopsidedly as non-imputation of sins, and therefore negatively, the emphasis in Thomas Müntzer is on effective righteousness, which is so important as to debar the Christian from 'boozing at Christ's expense'. Both as a fact and as a concept, Christ's representation retired increasingly into the background. On the left wing of the Reformation, soon driven into the underground of sects and groups, representation disappeared into discipleship, while the victorious right wing slipped back into the satisfaction theory of Christ's work.[1] It had not taken long for a purely moralistic and juristic view of imputation to reappear, regarding it as the imputation or non-imputation of something already given in advance rather than theologically as a creative utterance.

But this moralistic non-imputation destroys the ethical core

---

[1] See article 'Rechtfertigung' in *RGG*, 2nd ed. Vol. IV, col. 1755ff.

of personality, namely, responsibility. It was rightly criticized by the Enlightenment because of this, for reducing personal consciousness to the level of uniform indifference. To a sharpened ethical consciousness, divine imputation inevitably appeared to be a perversion of justice resting on an inherent irrationality. Such imputation is surely the destruction, the negation, of all morality.

Not surprisingly, the shelved problem of imputed righteousness reappeared just when the Enlightenment had passed its peak and was beginning to be criticized and eventually mastered and superseded, namely in German idealism.

In his early theological writings, dealing with Jewish positivism, Hegel had already put his finger on the central problem facing a doctrine of reconciliation in the post-Kantian period. Later he did so even more clearly in the third part of his *Lectures on the Philosophy of Religion*. Under the rubric 'The God-man and Reconciliation' he describes the sacrificial death of Christ, in contrast to the death of Socrates, as 'an act of absolute satisfaction'. But this is in the course of a critical discussion with a juristic thought pattern which cannot possibly provide a basis for representation. For law cannot possibly be the principle of divine imputation, since law holds each individual responsible for himself and his conduct.

> The fundamental objection to this idea (is) that each individual must take responsibility for himself, for his actions, that no one else can atone for him, nor he himself be absolved by such atonement. This is unquestionably the case from the standpoint of formal law, where the subject, the agent, is regarded as the individual person.[1]

Where this standpoint of formal law is made the basis of one's attitude—and it can be regarded as the Kantian standpoint as well as that of the whole social life of modern man—then 'the doctrine of moral imputation according to which each individual has to stand for himself only, and each is the doer of his own deeds'[2] continues to obtain. I 'am' my law, I 'am' what I

[1] G. W. F. Hegel, *Sämtliche Werke*, ed. Lasson Vol XIV, p. 158.
[2] *Op. cit.*, p. 172. ET Speirs and Sanderson, Vol. 3, p. 96.

do. From this standpoint the death of Christ can only be regarded as an 'alien sacrifice'.

From the standpoint of the ethical consciousness the only possibility is moral imputation—that is to say, accountability on the basis of the deed and its motive. Any other imputation, the non-imputation of sin for the sake of another, is 'alien'. 'Another has been punished simply for the sake of punishment, life has been negated, difference abolished.'[1] It seems on the face of it that imputation conceived in moral terms can only be suspended in theology at the cost of destroying the person as a responsible being.

But this means that a juristic view of representation based on such imputation of Christ's righteousness is still on the same level as the magical view, is indeed simply a rationalized version of the same thing, and is untenable if each individual is the agent of his actions. Hegel's term for this place where the subject 'stands as an individual person' is 'the field of finitude'. Here the unalterable law is that 'each individual at all events dies alone, and each must be and do what he has to do, alone and out of his own subjectivity and responsibility'.[2] Hegel regards it as of supreme importance not to injure the subjectivity of this legal consciousness, the acceptance of duty and responsibility, either by a magical view or by a juristic theology. The naive pre-moral idea of substitution would in his view be no answer. If Christ redeemed us at the price of our ethical consciousness and responsibility then it would be right to prefer damnation to the acceptance of such a gift.

But how then are we to understand an 'absolute satisfaction'? Hegel's answer is to point to the 'fate of Christ' which is in the sharpest contradiction to moral imputation. 'With the death of Christ, however, there begins the conversion of consciousness',[3] that is to say, of the merely moral consciousness. In the experience of reconciliation man reflects upon himself in an entirely new way, a way hitherto impossible while he was bound to the

[1] *Op. cit.*, p. 160, Vol. 3, p. 95.   [2] *Op. cit.*, Vol. 3, p. 95.
[3] *Op. cit.*, Vol. 3, p. 86.

principles of performance and law, and, in Hegel's phrase, 'fixed in finitude'. The new anthropology has left behind the 'field of finitude' where the subject stands along as an individual person and regards himself and is regarded by others as self-sufficient and non-representable. The conversion of the consciousness begins when man ceases to base his irreplaceability on his contribution alone.

The Spirit can 'make what has happened as if it had not happened' because it is 'known as free, as affirmative in itself' and has the power to change the 'qualities' and to leave behind the 'field of finitude'. Man is not exclusively what he does or has done. In his being—or, in Hegel's language, 'as Spirit'—he is related to Spirit, and his power to leave the field of finitude would be misunderstood were it regarded simply as the subject's own effort to lift himself out of the mire by his own hair. In the process of self-realization, the Spirit is the recognition of the new being which no longer derives its life from the substance of its deeds, but from the relation to the Spirit itself—the relation which Hegel calls 'differentiation'.

In other words, if God exists, it cannot be for man merely a question of morality—'the thinking and willing of the subject in itself or as starting from itself'. Morality and subjectivity are seen to be 'standpoints' of unreconciled subjectivistic finitude. If the individual really is 'for himself alone' then there is no room for 'God' in this standpoint. But what religion is concerned with is

an infinite relation to God, to God as actually present, the certainty of the kingdom of God, a sense of satisfaction not in morality, nor even in anything ethical nor in the conscience, but a sense of satisfaction beyond which there can be nothing higher, an absolute relation to God Himself.[1]

The deed and the guilt of the individual, the irrevocable past, cannot be stronger than—God.

Moral imputation would consequently be a denial of the God who 'can make what has happened as if it had not hap-

[1] *Op. cit.*, Vol. 3, qp. 87f.

pened'. It would mean stubbornly persisting on the field of finitude, blindly ignoring man's relation to something other, his existence in relationship to someone else. But if his existence in relationship to someone else now becomes more important to him than his past existence and deeds, then he ceases to be interested only in the conscience standing for itself alone. God really is greater than our heart and its moralistic, legalistic standpoint. The consciousness is raised to the standpoint of Spirit, henceforth sharing God's interests which are more important to it than its own. The imputation of Christ's righteousness in our favour rests on 'the Spirit' whose life is our life—our life which is no longer self-sufficient and no longer solitary.

Thus for Hegel, imputation is rooted in the one inalienable presupposition of his philosophy, the Spirit. Being infinite, the Spirit cannot suffer any limitation in actual finite man. But this basic presupposition was first made explicit and manifest in Christ, more precisely, in the 'satisfaction' achieved by Christ in his suffering and resurrection. The transition from mere man to the God-man takes place in the consciousness of the Christian congregation, which 'becomes certain of the union and unity of the divine and human nature'. Jesus revealed the reconciliation of God with the world. He did not appease God's wrath nor satisfy God's honour. Rather—in good Pauline language—'the history of God's appearing' consists, according to Hegel, in the fact that

God has shown himself to be by his very nature reconciled with the world, that what is human is not something alien to his nature, but that this otherness, this self-differentiation or finititude as it is sometimes called, is a moment in God himself, though to be sure a vanishing moment.[1]

The 'vanishing moment' in God, or 'this humanity in God' as Hegel says, by its otherness, by its strangeness, shows us the eternal history which God himself is, namely his self-differentiation 'and the removal of this difference'. God is this self-differentiation and its removal in reconciliation. This return

[1] *Op. cit.*, Vol. 3, p. 99.

of love is the Spirit. Jesus shows us that reconciliation is God's own free movement, but he does so not simply by teaching this (as if reconciliation itself were detached from him and simply the content of his teaching). On the contrary, by the very act of dying he reveals God's reconciliation in the otherness, in the strangeness of the human, which finds its ultimate expression in death. In Hegel's thinking, outmoded and legalistic versions of the imputation of Christ's righteousness are left behind. Kant had already eliminated the possibility of interpreting imputation in moralistic terms; but imputation itself was safeguarded in substance by Hegel, by being interpreted as the reconciliation of God with His otherness, as the taking up of the finite into the infinite.

I2

THE INCLUSIVE INTERPRETATION

HEGEL'S VIEW OF Christ's representation has two distinguishing features; firstly its theological suspension of morality, made possible by explaining the person in relational terms, and secondly its inclusive view of representation, which Marheineke[1] was the first to recognize as marking off Hegel's interpretation from earlier ones.

In Schleiermacher's doctrine of reconciliation too, the concept of representation is consistently interpreted as inclusive. Here the renewal of life is taken as the basis of reconciliation: Jesus is the prototype of a humanity directly related to God. In Christ, that is to say in solidarity of life with Christ, humanity becomes aware of what it can be, aware of the basis on which it can live—namely, 'the constant potency of His God-consciousness which was a veritable existence of God in him'.[2] In this respect Christ represents humanity coming to consciousness of its wholeness, and the representative satisfaction which he thereby made, while 'very easy to misunderstand', 'certainly cannot be thoroughly defended except on the assumption of a common life'. This 'common life' which for Schleiermacher is part of Christ's high priestly office, rules out an exclusive view of representation, 'in the sense that we are thereby relieved from the necessity of fulfilling it'. 'Indeed, Christ's highest achievement consists in this, that he so animates us that we ourselves are led to an ever more

[1] Philipp Konrad Marheineke, 1780-1846, a leader of the Hegelian school who edited an edition of Hegel's lectures on the philosophy of religion.
[2] F. Schleiermacher, *The Christian Faith*, ed. H. R. Mackintosh and J. S. Stewart, 1928. Reissued 1960, p. 385, Sec. 94.

perfect fulfilment of the divine will (John 15.2, 5, 8, 11).'[1]

The distinction between inclusive and exclusive representation was developed fully by Ritschl in his doctrine of reconciliation. Ritschl is critical of the traditional approach which sought to understand Christ with the help of Old Testament personal types. If we begin with the three offices of Christ as Prophet, Priest and King (a system believed to have had its first representative in Eusebius of Caesarea, but which only became influential in theology after the Reformation) then Christ's representation belongs to the *munus sacerdotale*, which traditional Lutheran dogmatics further subdivided into two functions: satisfaction and intercession.

But this figure of the priest who effects salvation by means of the atoning sacrifice—a figure foreshadowed in the sacred history—is calculated more than any other to betray us into exclusivist thinking. Only the priest, the consecrated person, may approach God. He alone can cross the particular barriers which are *tabu* for others. He does so as the representative of the worshipping community, which cannot do what he does and whose co-operation is excluded. As Ritschl sees it, the biblical material is clearly distinguished from this background of general religious history.

It is unbiblical to assume that any one of the Old Testament sacrifices after the analogy of which Christ is judged is meant to move God from wrath to grace ... It is unbiblical to assume that the sacrificial offering includes in itself a penal act, executed not upon the guilty person, but upon the victim who takes his place. Representation by priest and victim is meant not in any exclusive but in an inclusive sense. Because the priest draws near to God when he brings near the gift, therefore he represents before God those in whose behalf he is acting: it is not meant that because the priest and the sacrifice come near to God, the others may remain at a distance from God.[2]

What is true for the old covenant applies all the more to the

---

[1] *Op. cit.*, p. 456, Sec. 104.
[2] Albrecht Ritschl, *The Christian Doctrine of Justification and Reconciliation*, ET ed. H. R. Mackintosh & A. B. Macaulay, 1902, p. 474.

new. Ritschl's grounds for rejecting exclusive representation are akin to those of Hegel in rejecting 'alien imputation'. Reconciliation is not put on us like a new hat but on the contrary is, like *imputatio*, a 'being regarded differently' which results in a 'being different'. Representative reconciliation initiates transformation. If Luther, while unable to distinguish between imputed and effective righteousness, certainly distinguished both from a self-righteousness which we achieve for ourselves, then he too thought of representation in 'inclusive' terms, and he is not likely to be suspected of synergism! The important thing is not that Christ acted and suffered 'without us' but that we exist, act, and suffer in him. What is surprising is that Ritschl should so often have been accused of synergism precisely because of his inclusive understanding of representation.

If Christ by his obedience secures his nearness, his priestly relation, to God, that includes the intention that the existing and the future community should reach the same position. That is to say, Christ as a priest is the representative of the community which he brings to God through the perfect fulfilment of his personal life. This use of representation is inclusive, not, as it generally is, exclusive. The meaning of the idea is not, that what Christ does as priest, the community does not require to do; but rather that what Christ as a priest does, first in the place and as the representative of the community, there the community itself has accordingly to take up its position.[1]

When representation is interpreted exclusively, both reconciliation and responsibility are in fact misunderstood and devalued. Reconciliation is changed from an experienced personal event into an objective fact which must simply be taken note of. Responsibility melts away under the sun of 'cheap grace'. It is easy to see in exclusive representation the tendency to slip over into total substitution. A representative who represents exclusively will in fact replace the person he represents.

In contrast to that, how does Ritschl understand inclusive representation? We have seen that his view is not synergistic,

---

[1] *Op. cit.*, p. 546 (slightly altered).

unless we are to call existence itself, so long as it is not dead, 'synergistic'. Rightly understood, inclusive representation preserves the element of truth in the idea of exclusive representation —the truth, that it is not we ourselves who effect 'the ending of their separation from God, as the removal of that sense of guilt which is associated with distrust'.[1] God acts, reconciling the world to himself. But if our co-operation were for ever excluded, as a consistent exclusive interpretation necessarily assumes, then reconciliation would not be 'effective', declares Ritschl, with an obvious reference to the Protestant concept of *iustitia effectiva*. 'Their (i.e. the members of the Church) effective union with God is therefore to be thought of as the forgiveness of their sins.'[2]

Although Ritschl so clearly asserts that the removal of separation from God is God's own work, and his alone, it was always possible to accuse him of 'ethicizing' the Gospel and of synergism. For the following reason: while interpreting representation in consistently personal terms, excluding magic and substitution of any kind, he overlooked the other essential element, temporality. Formally, this comes out in his constant employment of negative terms to describe representative reconciliation, informing us of what it is not. It is not mistrust, not the sense of sin, not separation. But this removal, this negation of negation, is no more than a beginning. No account is taken of the positive truth which is involved here; the truth that Christ as our Representative secures us time. The future which Christ makes possible for us disappears into a kingdom of God which merely amounts to more bourgeois morality.

[1] *Op. cit.* p. 546f.
[2] *Op. cit.* p. 546.

13

BARTH'S OBJECTIVISTIC
INTERPRETATION

RITSCHL DID, HOWEVER—like Hegel at another level
before him—at least explore the possibilities of a personal
and non-substitutionary view of representation. Although
he related reconciliation consistently to the Christian congregation, it was no part of his purpose to minimize the irreplaceable individual and his unique being. He certainly failed to find
the appropriate concepts to express the personal, which, so to
speak, takes refuge in the ethical. This rescued for theology
the element of truth in the idealist thesis of the irreplaceable individual. The unfortunate impression that Christ is
simply a replacement installed by God to make up for our
failure to function properly (as if God were an impatient
employer) was avoided, at least until the great restoration
effected by dialectical theology. Such a conception is no less
absurd than the earlier notion that God required a whipping
boy.

Adapting a famous exclamation of the apostle Paul it might
well be said: 'O irreplaceable man that I am! Who will represent me?' The fact that it is so easy to misunderstand irreplaceability and to long for it as a quality which depends on a
particular contribution is no reason for denying its reality.
Theology achieves nothing by asserting that Jesus Christ is for
us if at the same time it treats the persons who are represented
as mere ciphers for whom the question of identity no longer
arises. In his *Church Dogmatics*, Karl Barth presents his view of
representation in a chapter entitled 'Jesus Christ, the Lord as

Servant'.[1] The obedience of the Son of God is described here as representation on our behalf. In harmony with Barth's christo-centric approach, all the emphasis is on the fact that what 'happened for us . . . happened without us'.[2] In other words, 'man can do nothing to help himself'.[3] Christ's representation is effective quite apart from what those represented do either then or subsequently. Christ 'has taken the place of us men, of many, . . . in order (there) to act in our name and therefore validly and effectively for us . . . representing us without any co-operation on our part'.[4] The New Testament prepositions accordingly

speak of a place which ought to be ours, that we ought to have taken this place, that we have been taken from it, that it is occupied by another, and that this other acts in this place as only He can, in our cause and interest, that we cannot add to anything he does there, because the place where we might do so is occupied by him . . .[5]

Barth's tendency is to objectify representation, to regard it as a fact which is independent of the assent or will of those repre-sented, as an 'in itself meaningful event', as a 'radical and total fact'.[6] The terms employed by Barth in formulating this radical view accordingly fail to indicate any distinction between re-presentation and substitution. Our place is 'occupied' by Christ. I have been 'relegated' by Christ and 'placed' in another sphere. Barth speaks of our 'deposition' and of our being 'forced'.[7] These are substitutionary terms. Barth equates re-presentation and substitution, and impelled by his objectifying tendency, turns Christ into a replacement. The relationship— established by the act of representation between Christ the Representative and us who are represented—is not conceived in personal terms. The man who occupies my place instead of keeping it open for me, who forces me instead of waiting for me, who acts totally and radically for me without me, has really no need of my agreement or even of my unexpressed (perhaps, in

[1] Karl Barth, *Church Dogmatics*, Edinburgh 1934ff, Vol. IV, 1, pp. 157-779.
[2] *Op. cit.*, IV, 1, p. 249 and frequently.
[3] *Op. cit.*, p. 251.   [4] *Op. cit.*, p. 230.   [5] *Op. cit.*, p. 230.
[6] *Op. cit.*, p. 231.   [7] *Op. cit.*, pp. 231, 233, 236.

view of my incapacity, inexpressible) wish. He needs no connection with me at all: regarding me, as he does, as someone to be replaced, and therefore as useless, incapable, or dead. Seeing my temporary incapacity, helplessness and weakness, he concludes that I am totally incapable. The very completeness of the representation, quite contrary to its nature, implies the complete incapacitation of man.

Involuntarily, irrespective of whether he wishes it or not, the incapacitated man is represented. Barth even cites Barabbas[1] as an example of Christ's representation.

The Jesus who was condemned to be crucified in the place of Barabbas stands on one side, and Barabbas who was pardoned at the expense of Jesus stands on the other; for he was not crucified, nor did he really contribute to his own liberation.[2]

On this view, no relation between the Representative and the person represented, between Jesus and Barabbas is necessary. It is impossible to find in the biblical text any idea that Christ died 'for Barabbas'—perhaps to save his life in the way that the friend, for whom Schiller went bail, wanted to die in the place of a certain tyrannicide. On the contrary, it is the 'people' who regard Christ as an acceptable substitute for Barabbas. But the concept of representation cannot be automatically applied in this way to any situation at all where for one reason or another one person replaces another. To depersonalize representation like this is almost to turn it into a stroke of luck—in this case, for Barabbas but not for the thieves crucified along with Jesus. Did Christ die any the less 'for them'? Can an act be detached in this way from its intention? Important as the truth is which Barth emphasizes—the truth that Christ died 'without us', and helpless as anyone is who needs representation—this helplessness and weakness cannot be absolutized without furthering the depersonalization of man. The represented here are simply replaceable pawns in God's chess game. Revelational positivism thus provides striking confirmation of the popular positi-

---

[1] Mark 15, 6-15.
[2] *Church Dogmatics* IV, 1, p. 230.

vism which regards the individual as no more than a replaceable machine component.

When we inquire into the philosophical presuppositions of this objectivizing interpretations, we discover once again that the missing factor is one of the *differentiae specificae* which distinguish representation from substitution, namely, the perspective of time. Representation regards man from the standpoint of time. It gains time for the man who is for the moment incapacitated. Substitution, on the contrary, is a spatial concept. In space, one thing can be replaced by another thing; in time, it is possible for one person to be represented by another person. It is significant therefore that in Barth's account of Christ's representation the keyword is man's 'place' (*Ort*). 'In that he takes our place, it is decided what our place is.'[1] Certainly Christ characterizes man's place as the place of sin. In carrying through his act of representation, Christ shows man up as a sinner, as one who wants to be judge but is in fact judged. Just by the fact that he was 'amongst us and lived and acted for us as the just or righteous man[2] Christ convicts man of being what he is. But this description of our place is only secondary and subordinate to the chief thing which Christ does for us—that is to give us time, new and real time for living, time which his representation makes available for us.

[1] *Op. cit.*, p. 240.
[2] *Op. cit.*, p. 257.

14

THE DIALECTIC OF DEPENDENCE AND RESPONSIBILITY
A Discussion of Bonhoeffer

BARTH'S INTEREST CONCENTRATES on the 'without us—for us' which absolutizes man's dependence at the expense of his irreplaceability and responsibility. This seems to suggest that we are dependent upon God but bear responsibility only for the world. In relation to God we need representation, but in relation to the world we ourselves are the representatives of the helpless. The question remains whether we do not misunderstand the dialectic of dependence and responsibility if we relate them respectively to God and the world in this fashion.

Are we in fact independent of the world? Do we not need representation here, too? This oversimplified scheme is orientated to a theistic conception of God, and bases its thinking, as it were, on the '*Deus nudus*', who confronts us directly and who puts our affairs to rights so that we in turn may order the affairs of the world. Having God behind him, man imagines he can assume responsibility for the world. But God is not 'behind us' but 'before us'. And no one who is dependent and aware of his helplessness can first make a declaration of independence, and then proceed to limit his dependence to what he calls God. Nor again is the world simply the object of our responsibility, providing material for our duty. Anyone who thinks in these terms necessarily removes redemption outside this world altogether. Whereas Barth thinks of representation as pure dependence without responsibility, the opposite danger of thinking of it as responsibilitywithout dependence seems to me characteristic of the other significant theological attempt in our century to reinstate the concept of representation, that of Dietrich Bonhoeffer.

If we disregard Bonhoeffer's first work, *Sanctorum Communio*, where representation is taken in the narrow theological sense of 'representation in relation to guilt and punishment'[1] and is discussed exclusively in terms of Christ's relation to us, Bonhoeffer's later statements move strictly within the sphere of ethics. In his *Ethics*, written more than a decade later and left unfinished, the concept of representation acquires greater breadth and plays an important role in the 'structure of responsible life'. Bonhoeffer's first concern is to eliminate the individualistic approach to ethics. He describes as 'fiction' the notion that 'the subject, the performer, of all ethical conduct is the isolated individual'.[2] Responsibility is a reality given in and with man's existence as social existence.

This principle is not affected by the extent of the responsibility assumed, whether it be for a single human being, for a community, or for a whole group of communities. No man can altogether escape responsibility, and this means that no man can avoid representation. Even the solitary lives as a representative and indeed quite specially so, for his life is lived representatively for man as man, for mankind as a whole.[3]

Bonhoeffer does not indeed attempt to understand this structure in anthropological terms, but explains it *a priori* in christological terms.

Jesus—the Life, our life—lived representatively for us as the incarnate Son of God, and that is why through him all human life is in essence a life of representation . . . Because he is life, all life is determined by him to be representation.[4]

This christological explanation remains obscure. It is simply taken for granted as being axiomatic. In phenomenological

---

[1] D. Bonhoeffer, *Sanctorum Communio*, 1963, p. 113 (translated from the 3rd German edition of 1960, the original first appearing in 1930).

[2] D. Bonhoeffer, *Ethics*, SCM Press, London 1955, p. 195; Fontana Library 1964, p. 224. (For the sake of clarity, the words 'representative', 'represent', 'representation' etc. have been substituted for other English equivalents—'deputy', 'deputyship' etc.—used in the official translation for the German *Stellvertretung* etc.)

[3] *Ibid.*   [4] *Op. cit.*, p. 195; p. 225 (Fontana).

terms, the statement would need to read: because all life demands representation, and without it hardens into a dead replaceable thing, Christ in meeting this demand is in fact 'the Life'. Bonhoeffer's thought does not move from below upwards, from the anthropological reality to the christological event. Indeed, he disqualifies such thinking as 'religious'. It is not simply that the method here is strange, requiring of theology prior acts of specific belief, but also that the method itself leads to material difficulties. For in Bonhoeffer's account, representation fuses with responsibility, and the other aspect of representation—dependence on a representative, a specifically 'religious' problem—is ignored. In that discipleship of Christ which means existing for the world 'in the complete surrender of one's own life to the other man',[1] representation means living one's own life.

Dependence, its indispensable correlate, vanishes, and the ethics of responsible representation must either be given a dogmatic basis—because Christ represented us, therefore our life is intended to be representation—or else it collapses into itself. But it is open to question whether a non-religious interpretation of Christianity, such as Bonhoeffer rightly called for, can confine representation to the field of ethics in this way. Does not this one-sided conception of representation as responsibility necessarily involve an 'above-below' structure interpreted non-dialectically, with the ones who are responsible always 'above' the ones not yet 'of age', those under instruction, are always 'below'? But this would surely destroy the very thing which the represented hope for and the genuine representative aims at, namely, the self-elimination of representation.

For, in the interests of the identity which still continues to be sought, the responsibility of the representatives automatically ceases with the response of the represented for whom they temporarily speak. Representation cannot possibly be conceived in personal terms without provisionality and temporariness. But those who think of it *merely* as responsibility too easily lose sight

[1] *Op. cit.*, p. 196; p. 225 (Fontana).

94

of its temporary character. The interests of the represented are constantly threatened by a transformation of responsibility into 'exploitation and tyranny'.[1] This danger that the responsible party will absolutize his own function was clearly recognized by Bonhoeffer, who therefore sought to limit responsibility in two ways. On the one hand, responsibility is limited by the neighbour, who is or who will become capable of personal responsibility; and, on the other, it is limited by God, who is the final judge of our actions and their unforeseeable consequences. This limitation, which Bonhoeffer calls 'correspondence with reality',[2] is intended to prevent responsibility from degenerating into manipulation, and representation into substitution. There is no such thing as 'absolute responsibility',[3] a responsibility without limits.

But is it really possible to mark off such limits—in God and the neighbour—objectively? The inadequacy of the idea of representation as mere responsibility is surely evident here. For responsibility leaves out of account the provisionality and dependence of the one who assumes responsibility. Even the responsible person can proceed as if the person for whom he has assumed responsibility were dead, and so replace him. This difficulty becomes apparent when Bonhoeffer speaks of the relation between the Church and the world, a relation which he describes as a 'twofold relation of representation'[4]. The Church 'stands at the point at which the whole world ought to be standing'. She serves the world as the means and instrument of proclamation. At the same time, the world itself is fulfilled in the Church, which is 'the goal and centre of all God's dealings with the world'.[5] Here again, therefore, the Church's provisional character is consistently overlooked because its representation is exclusively regarded as responsibility and not as self-eliminating provisionality. An unbroken line of representa-

[1] *Op. cit.*, p. 196; p. 226 (Fontana).
[2] *Op. cit.*, p. 197; p. 227 (Fontana).
[3] *Op. cit.*, p. 204; p. 235 (Fontana).
[4] *Op. cit.*, p. 266; p. 301 (Fontana).
[5] *Op. cit.*, p. 266; p. 301 (Fontana).

tively assumed responsibility leads here from God through Christ and the Church to the world. Obviously, this line, beneath its appearance of responsibility, at the same time implies a descending hierarchical order of importance. God makes himself dependent—therefore responsibility does not flow in one direction only, from above downwards, but in the reverse direction as well. So that the world in fact takes responsibility for God.

Bonhoeffer's failure to notice the structure of dependence, from which even the Church is not excluded, here produces unfortunate consequences. For this structure with its provisionality is actually the watchful awareness of the future *eschaton* protecting the Church from itself and from any temptation to absolutize itself. Of course the Christian community represents the world; at the same time it depends upon the world. It is not the world's culminating point, as if the empirical life of the congregation and the Church were the sum total of the world's hope! Representation is not to be conceived as detached from all eschatology, which is what Bonhoeffer does by interpreting it exclusively as responsibility. Only when representation is eschatologized, when it is therefore provisional, does it preserve the dignity of those entrusted to it. Only as we are aware of its eschatological and provisional character can genuine responsibility be saved from a complacent superiority.

For the Church's relation to the world is not simply one of 'serving'—a stance which subtly contrives to remain 'above' even when presenting itself as, and even believing itself to be, 'below'. A Church which never did anything but 'serve', and in doing so continually assumed responsibility for the world's affairs, would be incapable of dialogue with the world. It does not 'need' the world, except as an object of mission. Not being dependent upon the world, it can develop no solidarity with it. For a genuine dialogue, such attitudes as 'directing', counselling, pastoral care, would have to be abandoned or modified. For all these attitudes imply a concealed claim to rule, even (and perhaps especially) when they are spoken of as responsibility and service. Genuine representation contains a much deeper level of dependence and relativity than 'serving' ever reaches. The course of church affairs in the years following the Second World War demonstrates how dangerously Bonhoeffer's approach could be misunderstood and how easily 'serving' becomes a subtle form of domination.

The eschatological dimension is indispensable for representation. We experience representation, that is, we both look for it and practise it ourselves, in the hope of the new heaven and the new earth. But this must always mean—in the hope that representation will itself disappear. Representation preserves within itself the consciousness of non-identity, of distance. It is the acceptance of the difference—between identity and non-identity, home and self-estrangement, 'God' and world.

PART THREE

CHRIST THE REPRESENTATIVE
Sketch of a Post-Theistic Theology

'Jésus sera en agonie jusqu'à la fin du monde: il ne
faut pas dormir pendant ce-temps là.'

Pascal[1]

[1] *Pascal's Pensees*, ET Martin Turnell, 1962, p. 335; 'Jesus will be in agony until
the end of the world: we must not sleep during that time'.

15

INTRODUCTION

WHO AM I? How do I achieve identity? These questions almost
seem to have dropped out of view in the course of our theological inquiry into the treatment of representation in the Bible and
in tradition. Yet even when speaking of magical exchange or
voluntary suffering, of *satisfactio* and *imputatio*, of reconciliation
in alienation and of exclusive substitution in our place, it is indirectly we ourselves who are involved, since such concepts
describe the way in which the kingdom of identity is established.

The question which emerges from the tradition may be put
in this way: what do we mean when we say that we are represented by Christ in our actual situation? This question is not
answered simply by a reference to the relevant New Testament material as it lies to hand. Concepts like historicity,
universalization, voluntariness, and suffering, by themselves are no answer, for they can be interpreted very vari-
ously and our understanding of them can, and indeed must,
change if it is to remain valid. It is a truism to say that
the contents of the Christian tradition constantly need fresh
evaluation.

Radical criticism is all the more necessary in the case of a
concept like representation which from the beginning of Christian history has been threatened by magical and legalistic ideas.
The two conditions of genuine representation, personality and
temporality, were too easily lost sight of, with the result that
personality was depersonalized. The irreplaceable individual
became a mere pawn in God's chess game, and temporality
(the basis of the hope of the represented) was ignored in the

interests of a supra-temporal and timeless salvation mechanism, which lost none of its patent artificiality by being labelled 'salvation history'. We shall be saved from such fruitless re-pristinations if we begin instead with the phenomenon of re-presentation, with the preliminary understanding explained and discussed in Part One. Representation was seen there to be an inescapable requirement of the mind intent on identity. We adopted the Christian and idealist thesis of the irreplaceable individual and tried to keep firm hold of at least the *question* of identity, even though this identity is threatened today by complete interchangeability or 'substitution'. But irreplaceability can only be maintained at the price of dependence upon one who represents us. The very fact that a man's life is not completely contained in his present success or failure, but always includes an element that is still future, means that he needs representation.

From Hegel's anthropological approach, we learned that identity can only appear (and be conceived) in the difference between identity and non-identity. It is precisely this difference which explains both our *dependence upon* representation and our *responsibility for* representation. If representation is not to become substitution, and if the question about identity is not to be suppressed and hope in the kingdom of identity frustrated, two conditions have to be met—personality and temporality. In the light of these two conditions, so far defined only provisionally and superficially, we have now to examine more closely the structures of representation as lived and experienced. Our initial question was: who am I? The answer was: someone irreplaceable yet representable. The next question must be: who represents me? Or more precisely: who represents me without wanting to replace me? Who represents me in such a way that I continue to be counted on instead of being written off? Does representation, such as we hope for, exist at all?

The Christian faith answers all these questions by saying that from now on representation is not just a postulate of the reason, nor an everyday occurrence, but the really decisive event of all human history. Anthropology and christology are related as question and answer. In Tillich's terminology, they exist in correlation. To ask about the structures of living representation is necessarily to ask about Christ. In other words, it is to ask how we may define the representation which the concrete person Jesus (historicity) is said to carry out voluntarily for all (universalization).

Certain as it is that my quest for one who can represent me (and my possibilities) reaches out beyond the society in which I live, it is equally important for me as a person that this representative should not replace me. The answer given by the Christian faith to the quest for one who acts and suffers in my place is misunderstood if it is presented in perfectionistic and final terms. This tears identity and the kingdom apart. Identity degenerates into a substitutionary act on the part of Christ, and the kingdom of identity is postponed for ever. But Christ represents us only for a time, conditionally and incompletely. Christ does not substitute himself for us; he represents us for a time. And this must be maintained in opposition to all forms of christocratic perfectionism. We remain irreplaceable precisely because we need him as representative. He who in our place believes, hopes and loves—and who therefore does what we have failed to do—does not obliterate us so that nothing now depends on us. Christ does not replace our life, making us superfluous, not counted on by anyone any longer. Christological perfectionism turns Jesus, who is our brother, into a 'superman' who replaces us if this term 'superman' ever applied to anyone. But at the same time, this perfectionism turns God into an idol for whom man is exchangeable. But can it ever be a matter of indifference to God what becomes of me?

Any doctrine of representation which treats us, our sins, our history, as 'over and done with', not only destroys the irreplaceable individual but also abandons the God for whom men are not interchangeable. God, who despite the satisfaction already made, is still not content with the representative, continues to count on us, continues to look to us, to wait for us.

For him, our hope, which is fixed on him, is not detachable and already settled. God is *not* content with our representative. Our representative speaks for us, but we ourselves have to learn to speak. He believes *for* us, but we ourselves have to learn to believe. He hopes when we are without hope, but that is not the end of the story. The Spirit who intercedes for us with 'inarticulate groans'[1] does not intend to replace our own praying. But certainly he represents those whose only prayer is ignorance of what to pray for. By his representation he holds their place open for them lest they should lose it. Expressing it metaphorically, we need Christ so that God should not 'sack' us. Without Christ, God would dismiss us on the spot. Christ does not press for our dismissal, like some ambitious and more successful colleague. He is a representative, not a replacement. So God does not tear up our contract of employment.

But can this metaphorical statement be transposed into the realities of human history? Our 'place' or 'post' would in that case mean our freedom as God's children who have responsibility for the world. To say that because of Christ, God does not 'sack' us, means that he allows us this freedom so that we should no longer be the prey of mythical preconceptions and prejudices. The New Testament declares this freedom began in Christ: it is celebrated in the hymn to Christ in Philippians which the apostle derived from the tradition of the primitive Church. The cosmic powers—under, above, and on the earth—have paid homage to Christ.[2] It was all up with them as 'powers', as mythical, fateful forces, the moment they acknowledged Christ. They have lost the power to terrorize anyone. If at any time they are invoked, and appeal is made to their power (whether in the guise of blood and soil, party and state, or ministerial office and hierarchy), it can be pointed out that they have been disarmed. They now have to justify themselves as secular powers at the bar of reason, since no higher sanction can any longer be assigned them.

The recognition of Christ resulted in the abdication of the

---

[1] Rom. 8.26.   [2] Phil. 2.10.

powers. Once lords of the world, they no longer have any say. When man is still imprisoned in mythical thinking, he feels himself hemmed in by the world. He is caught in its toils, so it cannot become for him the medium of his self-realization. At the mercy of irrational powers, he remains a child, under age, immature. But Christ, the man of God, reveals in his life what liberation from these powers, which still boast of their invincibility, could be like. He demythologizes them. In mythical language, we express this by saying that he compels them to abdicate. In this way Christ ensures that we do not lose our 'post' as God's co-workers on earth. Without Christ, the earth would have been less subject to us, and consequently less habitable than it actually is. The freedom which dawned in him exists, of course, even where it does not appeal to him. Yet it can be said that his name is the indelible seal of this freedom. Whenever this freedom is threatened, whenever worldly powers, parading as myths, demand unconditional obedience, there too the secular consciousness is present in Christ's right and name. That, for the sake of Christ, God does not 'sack' us, then, means that he maintains in us this consciousness of freedom over against all such powers. By virtue of his radical freedom from every form of regimentation of the world, the 'place' promised us remains open—the 'place' of lords of the world, the 'place' *he* took in order that *we* might occupy it.

The engagement undertaken by Christ on our behalf can only be an incomplete and temporary representation, since it is on behalf of those who are and in Christ's view remain irreplaceable. Because Christ at no point sacrifices our identity to some higher goal, he necessarily acts for us 'incompletely'. Because we continue to be irreplaceable to God, Christ cannot sacrifice us to history, or to historical ends realizable only in the future—not even to a mythically interpreted final world judgment at the end of history. Representation is a kind of restoration of the damaged present, which is now once more given its due; something which is only possible, of course, insofar as the future is kept open for it. Christ does not include us all on one great account, for the simple reason that by representing us he shows that he expects more of us than we yet are.

He died for us—namely, in our place—but we too must learn to die. The Christian life is lived out as a learning to die in which physical death is only one, and that not necessarily the most concrete, form of dying. Using traditional language, we may say with Luther that this learning to die means acknowledging God's wrath as the truth concerning ourselves, and submitting ourselves completely to the dependence upon God implied in the concept of imputation. Of course, terms like 'God's wrath', 'dependence on God', require to be interpreted and translated into secular terms. This we try to do in what follows. It was for us, in our place, that Christ entered into life, but we ourselves have to learn to live. This means recognizing the human condition, and its characteristic estrangement, not as something alien to God but rather as a mode of His being with and among us. It also means perceiving identity in the non-identical—that is to say, living on the basis of this identity. The very goal of Christ's work would be destroyed if this work were in any way complete and perfect. Incompleteness constitutes the mode of his being for us.

In what follows, we examine the structures of Christ's representation in the perspective of this incompleteness. Christ's representation includes, of course, both the representation undertaken and carried out on our behalf in relation to God, and the representation of God to us. Three basic principles, already met with in Part One, seem relevant: identification, dependence, and provisionality. These must now be examined to see what light they throw on christology. The representation which we provisionally defined as 'personal' and 'temporal' will now be interpreted with the aid of these three concepts, which point to the fact that God does not suspend our freedom.

16

THE PROVISIONALITY OF CHRIST

A Note to the Dialogue with Judaism

THE TEMPORAL TERM to express the incompleteness of Christ's representation of us is provisionality. As our representative, Christ 'runs on before' us to God—he is our forerunner. The correlate of this provisionality of Christ (his 'running on before') is our discipleship (our 'following after') —our responsibility, *our* provisionality in the transferred sense of dependence upon the one who is before us. The life he already lives as existence in identity is for us still in the future, is not yet ours. But this non-identity first becomes aware of itself in relation to the identity which Christ provisionally portrays.

This is not to say that Christ is the precursor of someone greater, as was John the Baptist for example. Nor is Christ's provisionality the same as that of the prophets, who only expected the Messiah. It is an ultimate and final provisionality. To explain this statement it may be useful to recall the discussion between Jews and Christians which, in somewhat makeshift fashion, has been resumed in recent years. We Christians have every reason not to approach this dialogue as the ones who pose the questions, but as those to whom questions are put and who have much to learn. Whenever Judaism engages in self-examination, it invariably locates the decisive difference between itself and Christianity in the different view it takes of redemption. The 'essential conflict', according to Gershom Scholem,[1] is that in Christianity redemption is understood as

---

[1] G. Scholem, *Judaica*, Frankfurt, 1963. See the section on the interpretation of the Messianic idea in Judaism on pp. 7ff.

an event taking place in the spiritual realm, in the invisible world, and relates to redeemed individuals within an unredeemed world. In Judaism on the contrary, the visible world is the only conceivable scene for anything worth calling redemption ever to take place. The Jewish faith in redemption has never abandoned the stage of history, the world of public events, the medium of society. The messianic hope accordingly moves further and further away from the person of the Messiah and focuses on the new life which is to arise on earth.

The message of the *one* man, the Messiah, more and more takes second place to the message of the one time, of the days of the Messiah, and then alongside this, and even more definite message, that of the kingdom of God.[1]

Redemption is therefore not a perfectionistic once-for-all event but an unceasing process. 'The kingdom eclipses the Messiah.'[2]

The difference is an ancient one. It has proved important enough to settle whether a man should live or die. In the compulsory mediaeval disputations between Jewish Talmudists and Christian theologians, the Jewish scholars, standing in a single rank facing the ecclesiastical tribunal, took turns in answering questions posed by the theologians. Each time, the answer given could mean certain death for the Jew. In his novel *Le dernier des Justes*[3] André Schwarz-Bart tells how, in answer to a question about the divinity of Jesus, following a long pause, a timid Rabbi stepped forward and

with anxious little coughs and his voice on one thin note, whispered with constraint: 'If it is true that the Messiah of which our ancient prophets spoke has already come, how then do you explain the present state of the world . . .? Noble lords, the prophets surely stated that, on the coming of the Messiah, wails and moans would disappear from the world . . . ah . . . did they not? And also that all the peoples would break their swords, oh yea, and beat them into ploughshares . . . ah . . . would they not?' Finally the little Rabbi

---

[1] L. Baeck, *Das Wesen des Judentums*, Frankfurt, 1932.
[2] Sch. Ben Chorin, *Juden und Christen*, Berlin, 1960, p. 25.
[3] André Schwarz-Bart, *Le dernier des Justes*, Editions du Seuil, Paris, 1959: ET *The Last of the Just*, Secker and Warburg, London, 1961.

ventures to smile sadly at King Louis and say: 'Ah, whatever would people say, Sire, if you were to forget how to wage war?'[1]

For this answer, he is burnt in the flames in the name of Jesus Christ—because Christians, undeterred by 'the present state of the world', cling to the view that the kingdom of God appeared in Christ. It is essential to bear in mind the consequences of this and of every other form of Christian perfectionism when measuring the effect of ignoring the provisionality of Christ. A Polish Jew has declared that the name 'Christ' always makes him think immediately of *pogroms*. Theology cannot disclaim its responsibility here by dismissing such considerations as lamentable lapses in practice which cannot be laid at the door of the faith itself. The story of Christian antisemitism is too ancient, too uninterrupted, and too bloody to be evaded in this way. The least we can do for its victims is to re-think our Christian faith, for their sakes and in the light of their fate.

When we do engage in such rethinking, a final Christ—a replacement who perfectly and completely secures for us the reconciling grace of God—vanishes. That this final Christ is inevitably totalitarian is shown by the story of the Church's antisemitism, with its fluctuations determined by the dogmatic and political security of the Church at any given time. When things were going well for the 'new Israel', when the 'people of God' felt strong, antisemitism flourished, drawing its confidence from the security of hardened dogmatic positions. Among the decisions of the imposing Fourth Lateran Council of 1215 (a high water mark of the triumphal Church for which the suffering synagogue had to pay) were the late mediaeval dress regulations for Jews—and the doctrine of transubstantiation. The change of the eucharistic elements of bread and wine into the real presence of the body of Christ was elevated into a dogma on the basis of which all other religious customs were held to be illegal.[2]

[1] *Op. cit.*
[2] K. Kupisch, 'Das Christliche Zeitalter', in *Der ungekündigte Bund*, Stuttgart, 1962, p. 82f. Similarly W. Eckert, O.P., 'Kirche und Synagoge', in *Christen und Juden, Ihr Gegenüber vom Apostelkonzil bis heute*, ed. Marsch and Thieme, Mainz-Göttingen, 1961.

Christ's action for us therefore finds its completion in the sacrament: his sacrifice is the final substitute offered to God. The final Christ is explained theologically by the sacrifice repeated on the altar, by which God is appeased. But *love* cannot be appeased, even with sacrifice, so as to look for nothing further. Even if men forget the still unrealized kingdom of God because the sacramental presence of the final Christ fills their horizon, surely it is impossible to think of God as separated from this hope in his kingdom? The final Christ becomes a representative only in the limited juristic sense of one who has made reparation. The past tense is decisive. This representation, transformed into total substitution, can never again be called in question, no matter what the condition of the world may be. The sacramental Christ and the kingdom of God are identified. The *Christus prolongatus*, existing in the form of the Church, becomes a totalitarian institution in which the present crowds out any still open future. Those who have the final Christ need no future.

But a future is precisely what those who happen to be the underdogs and the also-rans at any given time need more than anything else. Their future is betrayed in the name of the final Christ, the very future which the provisional Christ keeps open for them. The concept of representation, rightly understood, could therefore well be the one best suited to do justice to the Jewish objection to the Christian view of redemption. For even if this objection cannot be refuted—least of all by Christian terrorism—the ground for it is surely removed permanently by the provisionality of Christian representation. In the provisional Christ, the kingdom of God is at the same time present and still not present. In the pure and limited representation of the One, who is now already where we have not yet arrived and who waits for us as the forerunner, there cannot possibly be any ground for the brash and confident Messianism which makes *pogroms* and courts of inquisition possible. The still invisible kingdom of God remains open as something still future rather than as something which already exists and has to be defended by all available means.

For the tension between the 'now already' and the 'not yet' is the tension between Christ and us whom he himself adopts representatively. G. Scholem defines the distinction between the Jewish and Christian views of redemption as one of orientation, in the one case to the visible, in the other to the invisible. What is the focus of faith? Is it really true that the Christian faith, unlike the Jewish faith, focuses on the invisible world? Surely this distinction is set aside in the representation carried out by One who is visible for others who are not now visible? The representative—of all men, not just of a particular people— performs the invisible work of redemption, but does so in order to make it visible. For the sake of the not yet visible he representatively confirms the invisible. He effects the individual—for only in this way can it be universal—reconciliation which is as yet neither public nor visible. But he does so with a view to reconciliation which is public, visible, and universal. This is the goal in view. The Christian assertion of the Messiah who has already come serves the Jewish assertion—namely, the open future of those who now need no longer to be their own 'sole' agents and guarantors. In other words, Christ enables non-Jews to become Jews; that is to say, he enables them to live in postponement.

Scholem says of Jewish history: 'It suffers the weakness of the temporary and the provisional which remains unrealized. For the Messianic idea is not simply comfort and hope. In all attempts to realize it abysses open up which draw all its forms down into absurdity. To live in hope is a magnificent thing, but there is something profoundly unreal about it. It devalues the intrinsic significance of the person, who can never find fulfilment, because the incompleteness of his undertakings devalues the very thing which touches the central value of the person. The Messianic idea in Judaism has necessitated a life in postponement, a life in which nothing can be done and accomplished in any final way.'[1]

But this life in postponement, in provisionality, so far from

[1] Scholem, *op. cit.*, p. 73f.

having been ended for Christians by the Messiah, is the very thing which the representative makes possible.

The representative who has degenerated into a replacement, a substitute, destroys the provisional character of reconciliation. He whitewashes it systematically for the Christian consciousness, and perverts it historically in Christian history, where the final Christ has again and again carried the day against the provisional Christ.

The practical importance of the question whether Christ is to be understood as final or provisional becomes clear when we consider the Church's empirical life and its possible form. In fact, for the Church's understanding of itself, everything depends on whether it recognizes the provisionality of Christ. If Christ provisionally represents us before God, this means that the company of believers must also take responsibility for someone before God. For the Church, this someone can only be the world, which the Church represents before God. It does so provisionally, conditionally, and for the time being. The Church is not a substitute with which God consoles himself for the loss of a world slipping from his grasp. On the contrary, where the Church really exists, God is assured of what is still future. The Church encourages God so far as the world is concerned, so that He does not give it up for lost but continues to count upon it. The Church exists wherever it emerges as the world's champion, not as its accuser; as its true spokesman, not as its denigrator. It accordingly knows and promotes the interests of its client. It effaces itself in everything which the world itself has meanwhile learned to understand and put into practice—in certain social tasks, for example. The Church can conceive a world in which it has itself become superfluous. The Church of the provisional Christ does not constantly need reassurance and confirmation—'Deliver us, guard Thy flock, help us'. Rather, the Church is open towards the God who becomes identical with Himself in the world.

17

CHRIST'S IDENTIFICATION WITH US

The True Teacher

WHEN WE SPEAK of provisionality we stress the distance separating Christ from us by virtue of the fact that he is in advance of us and already at a point we have not yet reached. If this distance were passed over, if that is to say, Christ occupied our place and replaced us, this would mean not simply the destruction of our irreplaceable being as persons but necessarily that too of the provisional world in which we live, in the sense of total substitution. We must therefore continue to keep Christ's distance from us in mind, but not undialectically. He does not replace us at the point we are at, since he is ahead of us, but neither has he run so far ahead that he can no longer, so to speak, look round on us. Running on before, Christ looks back at us. Provisionality and retrospection are inseparable.

Christ does not live a life of uninterrupted concentration on God. He is not a *homo religiosus* who exists in the world only for God and who is sustained and supported only by the 'absolute potency of his God-consciousness' (Schleiermacher). Such a Christ would still be a final Christ and not the provisional representative who exists for God in doing something for us. This is why all descriptions of Christ based on his unique consciousness of God are unsatisfactory. They ignore the other decisive characteristic of the representative Christ, namely, his continuing act of identification. He identifies himself with those who follow after, those who remain behind, those who no longer move forward. He identifies himself with those whose identity is still future. The basis which makes this dialectical refracted

identity of ours possible is the act of identification carried out in
our interests by one who is ahead of us in the sense of having
already achieved identity.

But what does identification mean? In what sense can it be
said of someone that he identifies himself with another, for it is
surely undeniable that guilt and death and even pain and
punishment are not transferable phenomena? What does it
mean to say that he 'bore our griefs' and 'took our iniquities
upon him'? What kind of identification does this presuppose?
Our conception, shaped as it is by consciousness of the self, sees
the body as clearly defined in space, whereas, in societies where
totemism and magic in the broader sense play a role, another
less differentiated sense of the body has been developed. In the
realm of the 'omnipotence of thoughts', not only is it theoreti-
cally possible for a man to identify himself with another's pain
so as to take it from him and die of it—it is also a demonstrable
fact. We meet a similar phenomenon in the field of psychoan-
alysis where the practising psychiatrist falls ill. But these possibilities are in general remote from our experience and not
reproduceable by us. In our experience nothing is as unmistak-
ably our own as physical pain. However strong our desire may
at times be for such mythical exchange, especially in relation to
someone we love, we none of us escape this differentiation of
one person from another through the body, or rather through
our experience of the body. Such exchange is denied us. The
pattern of mythical identification, which can even dissolve the
barrier of death, certainly reminds anyone who hears of such
representation, of the unconscious omnipotence of thoughts in
dreams and of the identity attained in and through identification. But this hint given by the unconscious only makes us feel
helpless and sad, for it is a hint we cannot follow up.

We seem to glimpse a reflection of human self-identity when
the identification of one irreplaceable person with another
appears possible. What appears here, as in a mirror, is expressed in Christian anthropology (for example in Paul's idea
that knowing is a being known, loving a being loved) in the

statement that identity is only attainable by someone with whom another identifies himself. Identity is not achieved nor created, not even when it is explained in psychological terms as self-acceptance. For I am only able to learn to accept myself in my social, personal, historical situation (in my own case as a German, a woman, a person of average ability) if somewhere and at some time I have already been accepted. So long as no one else accepts me, self-acceptance is impossible. When someone identifies himself with me, this does not mean that he accepts me occasionally and on certain conditions. Identification is the readiness to accept without limit, without conditions. It means acceptance as a matter of course. But is there in this disenchanted world a pattern of such identification with another —one which includes the elements of responsibility and risk, failure and punishment, pain and suffering? Such a pattern does indeed exist, but it has been completely mishandled in theology and almost changed out of recognition by controversy. It is the pattern of the teacher.

The Enlightenment's idea of Christ as a teacher of virtue, happiness, and immortality has been dismissed as inadequate by modern theology. A Christ who was 'merely' a teacher was beneath the notice of many theologians, especially those of the dialectical school. Such superiority was justified so long as men thought of a teacher as a person of exemplary moral character who conveyed to others various kinds of information. The moralistic scheme on which the pedagogics of the Enlightenment was based regarded the teacher merely as a model of virtue and a conveyor of knowledge. But this was an astonishingly shallow conception of a calling which surely retains a far greater wealth of meaning than customary images, such as shepherd or king, which were taken from the world of the Old Testament and applied to Jesus. As if the reality denoted by the term 'teacher' were even remotely covered by a definition which limited itself to describing him as an example of kind, gentle, self-disciplined behaviour. And, in addition, one who conveys certain intellectual goods!

A teacher who does not also give himself—in, with, and under the facts which he conveys—is not a genuine teacher. A teacher who could be replaced by a learning machine would be better replaced. Indeed, the increasing rationalization of the learning process by means of technology focuses attention all the more on the need to personalize the teaching process. To describe it as 'setting an example' is inadequate. The one indispensable thing is the teaching act itself, the basis of which is the teacher's identification with his pupils. The teacher is responsible for those who are still immature or incapable. He safeguards the opportunities and interests of those he represents. He knows more about them than they know themselves. His (provisional) representation extends concretely to the place the pupil in his ignorance has not yet reached. The very provisionality of the teacher's action ensures that the pupil's opportunities, as yet unknown, will not be wasted. He secures for the maturing child the delay it needs. He thereby keeps the pupil's 'place' open for him. The educational process attains its goal when the pupil achieves identity, when he finds his 'place'. A teacher who does not efface himself, does not remove himself, make himself super-fluous, is not a good teacher. Obviously this removal does not happen all at once, in the way a pupil reaches the end of a parti-cular grade, but is a continuous process in the course of which the teacher time and again withdraws himself and makes him-self superfluous. The art of teaching is essentially this with-drawal and self-effacement, based on the prior identification of the teacher with the pupil.

We can apply this pattern of the teacher to Jesus. He is the one who identifies himself with us, who in our interests secures us time and delay. It is very easy to picture Christ as the 'eternal' teacher whose work is never done, and who thus never becomes superfluous. To this conception corresponds the picture of man as the 'eternal child', which is not made more acceptable by speaking of him as 'God's child'. This unexamined father-child relationship in the form in which it has too long dominated theo-logy was orientated to a patriarchical society ruled by tradition.

When God was father, all men were also children. But God is no king, he is Spirit. God is no father, He is Spirit. He wants us to be men and women, not children . . . A new tremendous theme presents itself which must be delineated, penetrated with our minds, expressed, explored: the theme of man with head held high.[1]

The dominating father-figure—transferred from God to the ruler and to the head of the family—allowed the child only one possibility of identity, filial piety. Responsibility for the world, the liberty of the sons of God, proclaimed with astonishing boldness in the New Testament, vanished from view.

But even the best father-child relationship cannot remain unchanged throughout life except at the price of degenerating into a mutually engendered tyranny and childishness. It is Christ's express intention not to keep us at the level of immature children, as if he were an 'eternal' (and therefore a bad) teacher. He wants us in our 'place' as God's fellow workers,[2] as heirs of the world,[3] as those called to the freedom of the sons of God.[4] It is Christ's declared will that we should graduate from his school to his kingdom. This is why the Jesus of the synoptic gospels speaks so little of himself. Whatever view we may take of their historicity, Jesus' sayings about himself are far outnumbered by the host of sayings about the kingdom. This is the mark of the true teacher. He does not push himself, his own person, the need for loyalty to himself, into the centre, however true it may be that such loyalty follows precisely when it is not insisted on. What is binding on his followers is his cause, his kingdom.

The Problem of Punishment

Being a teacher does not simply mean teaching this or that subject, it means self-identification. And there is a yardstick for measuring the degree of identification in a given case: the

---

[1] Thornton Wilder, *Kultur in einer Demokratie*, Frankfurt-am-Main S. Fischer Verlag 1957. Original in German.

[2] I Cor. 3.9.　　　　　　[3] Gal. 3.29.　　　　　　[4] Rom. 8.21.

teacher's attitude to punishment. How does he justify the infliction of punishment and what therefore does he regard as the
appropriate form of administering punishment? Two possible
explanations of punishment hold the field today. They are in
dispute, and can acquire importance for theology according as
the latter is orientated more to law or to pedagogy. The expiation theory asserts that punishment safeguards the dignity of
the wrongdoer because it alone takes his personal responsibility
seriously. Leniency or pardon would fail to respect his freedom
and responsible being as a man. The upholders of the rehabilitation theory, on the other hand, begin with the disturbed relationship already existing between the individual and society
before any crime is committed. Once the crime—which itself
is a symptom of the disturbance—has been committed, society's
duty is to reintegrate the criminal. On this view, punishment is
an educative process. In a theological concept of punishment
(punishment decreed for us by God and accepted by Christ)
only the former theory of punishment as expiation has hitherto
played any role. It encounters difficulties of course, once the
metaphysical framework, the notions of hell and heaven, is
destroyed. Or at least it become so questionable that practical
human problems, such as capital punishment, can no longer be
decided on the basis of notions of this kind which have become
detached from their framework. Because of its difficulties with
punishment, theology tends increasingly to be silent on this
theme. (The kind of dispute about the duration of the pains of
hell which stirred Leibnitz would be inconceivable today.) But
it is doubtful if theology can in fact dispense with an understanding of what was traditionally known as 'hell', and a post-
metaphysical interpretation of 'hell' cannot ignore the general
post-metaphysical view of punishment.

Both contemporary theories of punishment are relevant for
theology. A statement like 'upon him was the chastisement that
made us whole' actually points more to rehabilitation than to
expiation. The peace of God involves our reintegration into
society. Christ re-socializes us, that is to say, makes us citizens

of his kingdom. Just because we are citizens, we are not exempted from responsibility, like persons discharged on the grounds of diminished accountability.

As a true teacher, Christ administers punishment very differently, of course, from one who is simply a judge. The difference between the two typical figures is seen in their relationship to the person being punished. This can be illustrated by an example from recent educational theory: Makarenko's theory of punishment.[1] According to Makarenko, the infliction of punishment is only meaningful if the person who inflicts it himself suffers under the punishment he sets. Any other kind of punishment—that imposed by the teacher without himself feeling its severity—is sterile. It must 'cost' the educator as much as the pupil—for example, in time lost with a pupil kept in after school hours. In this view therefore, punishment is not something imposed by a subject upon an object, but a personal transaction which affects not only the individual being punished but those related to him as well, since we can never think of him in isolation. This identification on the part of the teacher who acts representatively abolishes the difference between the agent and the acted upon.

A moment's reflection on this view of punishment is enough to show its cleansing and clarifying effects when applied as a touchstone to the structure of Christian dogmatics. For the main difficulties in the older approach, whether by way of a theory of *satisfactio* or of a theory of expiation, lie in the concept of God as the 'old oriental' (Nietzsche) who wants or is driven to punish at all costs, and for whom everyone is 'just' so long as the required penalty has been paid. When punishment is seen from the standpoint of the injured good (as it still is by Anselm) rather than as the restoration of a broken personal relationship, this inevitably gives rise to all those strange theological controversies about law or grace, God's justice or Christ's mercy, which land us in an artificial yet irreduceable tension. When

[1] A. S. Makarenko, *Ein pädagogisches Poem*, in *Werke*, Berlin, 1958, Vol. I; and in *Ein Buch für Eltern*, *Werke*, Vol. IV.

God has to look to his honour, then the agent and the acted upon continue to confront one another irreconcilably in a system of domination and servitude. But this system collapses when the Lord identifies himself representatively with the servant. A real identification is only possible when the one who punishes suffers no less under the punishment than the one being punished. Representing us provisionally, Christ punishes us in such a way that he suffers himself. That is just what being a teacher means.

If the theological concept of punishment is not to lag behind the humanity of Makarenko's understanding, it will not restore the master-slave pattern which has been abrogated by Christ. The term 'punishment' could indeed easily mislead us into a metaphysical error, as if the term referred to an educational device which God needed in order to assert himself. But what meaning can the punishment decreed and borne by identification have, if it is no longer possible to give it a post-mortal significance? The view taken here of the punishment by God of the sin of the world is that it consists in the historical consequences of definite attitudes and actions of the consciousness.

Whatever we do or even merely think, changes the world in which we live, reshapes it. For these intended or unintended consequences we are responsible. The altered world in turn operates on us, forcing us for example into the political causal nexus of guilt (German), retaliation (Polish), and revenge (German). This influence, which limits our choices even before we perceive them, we call 'punishment'. On this view, the agent of punishment, the punishing God, is nothing other than the whole complex of social relationships. Whoever sows the wind reaps the whirlwind.

No other, no metaphysical view of punishment is any longer viable. Nor would such a view include more than is already included in this 'metaphysical' totality of social relationships. And anyone who thinks this statement is simply an evasion, anyone who thinks that God is bound to punish in some absolute fashion, is treating the deadly cycle of social and individual consequences far too lightly. If we can no longer speak today of God's wrath and of his being our judge—in the sense of a supernatural intervention either within history or after death—then Sartre's definition of hell as 'other people' is an apt theological description. It indicates a profounder knowledge of God than they have who keep quiet about hell just because they can no longer speak of it in metaphysical terms.

In this concrete worldly form, punishment is seen in the fact that those who destroy hope live themselves in an atmosphere of hopelessness. What they imagined they were inflicting on others they were really inflicting on themselves, and it marks them out. The curse of the evil deed is that it recoils upon the world and the 'I' inexorably. The liar deceives himself, the man who treats other men as prisoners is himself imprisoned. The loveless are bored; and there is no need for any worse form of punishment, perhaps in some post-mortal hell, than this abandonment to a world thus produced and determined. Throughout his life each receives according to what he is. Christ did not abrogate or pronounce invalid this law of the hell which is 'other people', of the hell which I make for myself, this law which Paul called the law of 'sin and death'. On the contrary Christ fulfilled this law, by his identification. He was born 'under the law',[1] he identified himself representatively with those who are subject to its deadly cycle.

If we understand Christ as the true teacher, his being as judge and his decreeing of punishment are included in this being as teacher. He punishes us in such a way that he suffers himself. He identifies himself with the life of those who are condemned for life. He suffers everything which results from the destruction of hope. The Lamb of God who 'bears' the sin of the world is the man of God who 'bears' the world's inhumanity: that is, the consequences of the world's sin—destruction. Christ's entire life is determined by this unending identification with those who are the agents of their own punishment. Christ makes the prison warders aware of the prison in which they

[1] Gal. 4.4.

themselves live, and he does so by showing that he *himself* is its prisoner. He identifies himself absolutely, without prior conditions, without restrictions of class, race or sex. In this identification the relation of agent and acted upon is abolished. Christ belongs to both parties at the same time; he punishes and is punished. He thereby excludes any idea of punishment as a predetermined fate. It ceases to take by surprise those on whom it falls, as if it were something meaningless, for the judge identifies himself with the condemned, the teacher shares the punishment alongside the pupil.

This does not mean that by this identification Christ and those he represents fuse into simple identity. Identification makes identity at a distance possible. The identical one is at the same time the non-identical one, and it is only on the basis of this non-identity that he acknowledges and imposes punishment. The dialectical relation between teacher and pupil is one of identity in non-identity, of 'one-ness in separateness' as the young Hegel formulated it. As teacher—or precursor—Christ has reached a different stage. But his sharing of the punishment, his identification with the botched cause of the other person, makes him into a servant who takes responsibility and suffers. Only in and through this identification, by another, with his own botched cause can the pupil learn to identify himself with his own cause. But this means learning to accept punishment. Because Christ identifies himself with us, in teaching and in punishing, he enables us to accept ourselves as guilty but also to be at peace. He is the link between the two proposed explanations of punishment: expiation appears in the consciousness of non-identity and peace in the process of reintegration in society. In Christ's representative identification we have identity in non-identity, that is to say, peace with God.

18

CHRIST'S DEPENDENCE ON US

PROVISIONALITY AND IDENTIFICATION are marks of the representation Christ carries out on our behalf 'before God'. Both characteristics are intimately connected with a third, namely, the representative's dependence on those he represents. In all that Christ does, he has, as representative, made himself dependent on our assent. Representation can only be thought of as a conditional, and not as an automatically effective event. Christ acts in our place conditionally, aware that we think of, and reject, his way of representing our life as absurd. Like every other representative, Christ depends on our yea or nay, on our assent, otherwise he would merely be a replacement.

Christ's dependence is the presupposition of his suffering. He 'depends on', is conditioned by, the sadism of the bored occupying troops. He 'depends on', is conditioned by 'my sins' which fell upon him. So complete is his identification with our real life that it will never be possible to speak of him alone, in himself, apart from his success or failure. He depends on what we make of him. Our acceptance of his identification, which is the object of his 'sacrifice', is by no means so secured in advance that we are 'healed' as it were simply by virtue of a mechanically operating salvation history. Christ puts himself at risk— his life, his work, his cause—by making himself dependent on us. We may even say that he puts his God at risk, for he makes the truth of this God depend on our assent.

Only within the limits of this dependence can we speak seriously of Christ's sufferings. Dependence and the capacity to suffer are intimately related. The non-dependent person does not suffer. So it is utterly wide of the mark to interpret Christ's suffering as stoicism. *Ataraxy*, the stoic virtue of indifference, may be the appropriate term when the body alone suffers, while the soul is independent and free of merely 'external' happenings of this sort. In that case, nothing is really in jeopardy, except that the hero may lose face. For stoic endurance, there can be no question of suffering 'for' others. We have to distinguish between suffering which is probationary, intended to test and in the end to vindicate a man's constancy; and, on the other hand, the situation in which someone is delivered up to suffering as Christ was, without any way of escape into some inner sovereignty. In the case of the stoic hero or martyr, the cause of his suffering is irrelevant, being unrelated to its purpose. Not so for Christ! He suffers 'for us', by suffering because of us. Which is why, as Pascal says, he will 'be in agony until the end of the world'. For Christ no retreat into himself, into his personal dignity or attitude, was possible; but only a 'remaining under' (which is what the New Testament word for 'patience' literally means); only the dependence of the representative who has surrendered himself without remainder. Christ reserves nothing of himself to fall back on, to retreat into. He does not even have 'God behind him' to allow him to be indifferent whether the world raged or rejoiced. Even for Christ, God is the coming one still awaited. In the Christian view, suffering is always the surrender both of self *and* God.

Without this suffering which is rooted in dependence, representation is inconceivable—except in a magical or substitutionary sense. The *ushabti* help the dead person, not by their 'fear and pain' but independently. The replacement or substitute, as well as those who are replaced, cannot see any other possibility outside this choice between being everything or nothing. The mediating situation of the one who is provisional, alive, and capable of suffering, is ignored by them.

The person who represents someone, and so makes himself dependent, must be prepared for the worst. One who identifies himself can no longer be free to choose the time and place of the identification. If he once withdraws he ceases to be identified; if he once refuses to be involved, he has refused ever to be involved. The forerunner is shown up in all his provisionality when no one follows him. This is precisely the way Christ, the teacher, the forerunner, puts himself at risk. This doctrine of Christ's continuing, representative suffering is contested by those who regard the resurrection rather than the cross as the central event which forms the basis of the Christian faith, and who see the resurrection itself as God's final victory over his enemies and not simply an anticipatory sign of hope. For them, the cross on which Christ puts himself at risk, is simply an event in history, a transitional stage, ended by the power and glory of God. For them, the reality of history is prefigured in Easter, and from Easter dates the rule of Christ.

But this means that nothing unexpected can now ever happen in the world's history, nothing which was not already provided for in the divine plan of salvation which Easter unveiled. History becomes simply the unfolding of the predetermined. Admittedly the individual can still forfeit his share in the revealed salvation, can still contract out of it. But this no longer makes any essential difference to a world which in principle is already redeemed. It is therefore of little consequence whether we describe the time which continues after the resurrection as a development, or a process, or even as the 'end of history' (Bultmann) which has taken place in Christ. In any case, the historicity of man has been abandoned in the light of this Easter reality. For historicity, as a basic experience of modern life, can be defined as man's 'standing at risk' in time. Man can forfeit and botch his own life, and the life of the world too—that world of which he is lord, in the New Testament sense of maturity and responsibility. Man does not 'possess' himself as a self-evident being in contrast to everything else which exists. On the contrary he is continually projecting himself afresh. This experimental character of man's life is only preserved within the perspective of a world in which the resurrection is simply a sign of the dawn, a pledge of redemption,[1] and not the manifested reality of redemption.

We still hope in Christ's resurrection as the achieved identity of all men, but we do so not because the final Christ has withdrawn us from the complexities of the world and the risks of history, but because the provisional Christ hangs on the cross of reality even to the end of man's days. Only here, on the cross, does Christ identify himself with the fears and sufferings of those whom God has forsaken, with the sin of those who have forgotten God, and with the destruction of the world, which is the inner logic of this sin. Christ's resurrection did not abrogate this law of the world—the law that love itself is destroyed, when it identifies itself with those who are destroying themselves, into something higher and more perfect. What the resurrection did was to give that law universal validity and embody it in a visible sign. When the message of Jesus entered the world, as a result of what his disciples experienced as his resurrection, the historic person of Jesus became the Christ of faith, whose cross on Golgotha now casts its shadow over the whole world. In the symbol of the resurrection, this shadow of the cross so imprinted itself in reality, that it can never again be forgotten as the key concept for the objective onlooker and as the possibility of life for those who accept this identification of another with themselves.

[1] Eph. 1.14.

19

'BEFORE GOD'

IT SHOULD NOT be necessary to add any special reference to
the basic characteristic of Christ's representation, because it is
already implied in the marks of provisionality, identification,
and dependence—namely, that Christ represents us 'before
God'. Either this characteristic was assumed in what has been
said and cannot add anything new to it, or everything said so
far is unimportant and secondary and would need to be radically revised. If the qualifying phrase 'before God' is not
implicit in the statement that 'Christ represents us' then the
addition of the vocable 'God' will be merely rhetorical. Where
this representation takes place, God (if not in the direct sense
of religious object) is present; and he is being spoken of even if
his name is not mentioned. All the anthropological characteristics we have described—that man needs a forerunner if he is to
gain an extension of time; that man acquires identity through
the identification of another; that when he acts representatively
he makes himself dependent and suffers, because he puts himself at risk all these statements speak of God, and do so in fact
in the only possible theological sense by speaking of what God
does in us. The Christ—who represents us before God—accepts
himself as a provisional Christ, lives in the provisional, and puts
us into the provisional, so that we are able to accept ourselves.
But acceptance of oneself, as one who lives in postponement,
means nothing else except running ahead 'to God' and knowing that one's real life or identity is in him. What is known to be
in him, saved in him—namely, our identity, which is not here
but from which we derive the strength to deny plainly and

definitely what actually *is* given—is symbolized in Christ. Christ represents our irreplaceable uniqueness, the 'infinite worth of the subject'. But just as surely as he does this 'before God'—in other words, unconditionally—so just as surely do the structures in which representation is expressed (provisionality, identification, and dependence) imply no direct and in that sense religious relation to God.

Christ, who represents us, makes himself dependent upon us. He puts himself in our hands, since on us depends the success or failure of his enterprise. But just by putting himself in our hands, he puts himself in God's hands. For there is only one way to make oneself dependent on God and that is to make oneself dependent on men. We can only surrender ourselves to God when we surrender ourselves to men. Any direct surrender to God, such as the saints of the great religions exemplify, is no longer possible for us in this post-theistic age. For us God is not directly present. His great incognito—'the least of these my brethren'— is now irrevocable, and we have no grounds for complaint on this score. For Christ is in fact the beginning of this stage, when God is represented by the man who exists for other men, and when surrender to men always involves surrender to God. Christ, who represents us, identifies himself with us. This identification with another rests, in fact, on identification with God. Once again, there is no other identification with God —no, so to speak, more direct, more divine identification with him. For if, in and with the reality of identification, this radical existence for others is given, then there is nothing that we could be or do for 'God': nothing over and above this radical existence for others. God has made himself implicit in our history. It certainly appears as if certain direct forms of religious life remain untouched by the changes of a history in which God still only appears indirectly. Prayer, especially in the form of pure adoration and praise, seems to be one such survival of a direct relationship to God. Yet even here, in the case of prayer, it remains true that, whatever may be the forms in which it survives in a post-Christian age, the reference made in prayer to

God's future has its starting point in identification with the world in which we live. Prayer summons God into this world; but this summons is only a call to God when it remains faithful to the earth. Otherwise it is simply a cry for a substitute satisfaction, for a sedative—in short, for compensation. Prayer is 'before God' only when it is in the world.

Christ is provisional—if we add 'to God' we emphasise the provisionality but say nothing new.

Christ makes himself dependent on us—if we say 'dependent on God', this simply means that Christ is radically surrendered to men.

Christ identifies himself with us—if we add 'before God' it amounts to the same thing, for whenever this *identificatio* takes place, God is there.

20

THE DEATH OF GOD
AND THE PROVISIONALITY OF CHRIST

CHRIST IS NOT only our representative before God, he likewise is God's representative among men. This representation of God by Christ has, of course, frequently been the theme of dogmatic explanation and theological reflection in Christian history, but always only from standpoints which begin from God's side. It is God who imparts himself in Christ, God who reveals himself in Christ. The real subject of what theology calls 'revelation' or 'incarnation' is God. It is he who acts. But though the New Testament contains abundant testimony to the truth that Christ represents God and acts in his stead on our behalf, this has never been developed in dogmatics from the standpoint of representation. Representation was restricted exclusively to Christ's action and suffering in our stead, while his representative action and suffering in God's stead was ignored.

One dimension of christology was thus lost from view. The reason for this omission is probably to be sought in the theism which theology up to now has more or less taken for granted. So long as God 'lives'—so long as men can say, 'And a God exists! A holy will lives!'—there is no compelling theological need to reflect upon Christ's representation of God as the representation of one who is absent. For long enough God was known as absolute immediacy, more certain even than one's own self. All previously known forms of the Christian religion have presupposed a direct relationship to God, and are therefore in jeopardy the moment God ceases to be needed as a working hypothesis in morality, politics and science. They are undermined when fate no longer strikes its blows at man directly through natural phenomena, when the age-old experience of man's exposure to the forces of nature becomes less direct and is robbed of its force by the achievements of medical science, world trade, and planned (in theory at least) political change. Religion is undermined because in a technological world God loses ground at an accelerating rate. The impression arises that God has been thrown out of work, for society removes one area of life after another from his control. It can be said that in the wake of the Western European Enlightenment the self-evident existence of God has been destroyed for the whole world. Naive theism, a direct childlike relationship to the father above the starry sky, has become impossible. Any direct religious certainty has also become impossible, though this should not mislead us into speaking of the end of religion altogether. Any metaphysical 'positing' of God which, by appealing simply and naively to the 'fact' that God is alive, ignores the 'most important of more recent events—that "God is dead" '.[1] To adopt such an attitude is to remain a prisoner within the private sphere of individual religious aptitudes and experiences.

It is in this condition of the consciousness, in the post-theistic age, that the truth that Christ represents the absent God first takes on its full significance. Only when the self-evident character of God is finished with does the miracle of Jesus of Nazareth shine out, the miracle that a man should lay claim to God for other men by representing him. As in any bereavement, the challenge presented us by death can be met in two ways. Either we can assume that God's absence means he is dead, and so seek or create a substitute for him. Or we can regard his absence as a possible mode of his being-for-us. In either case, God's role is not left unfilled. It is obvious that society, with its rationalization and technical capacity in the broadest sense, has taken over many of the main functions of the God of previous periods. It is clearly well placed to perform these functions

[1] Friedrich Nietzsche, *Complete Works* (ed. Levy, T. N. Foulis), London, 1910, Vol. 10, *The Joyful Wisdom*, p. 275.

which previously were assigned to God. Indeed, in some re-
spects—for example, in providing an explanation of the world,
in healing the sick, in affording protection against disasters—
it is in a better position to do so than the God of former ages, so
often appealed to in vain. But it is just as obvious that the substitute which society offers for God is incomplete. Society is
unable to satisfy a religious longing which always reaches beyond it, the longing for meaning and purpose in life, the longing for personal identity and for the kingdom of identity. The
unresolved problematic character of an absurd situation mid-
way between meaninglessness and the longing for meaning
forces us to the non-logical conclusion that God must be represented.

The absence of God can be interpreted as one mode of his
being-for-us. In this case, man depends on there being someone
to represent the irreplaceable God. Nietzsche's statement that
'God is dead' is then transposed into the requirement that
'God must be represented', an idea not so very remote from the
Nietzsche who could speak of God's 'sloughings'. To say that
God must be represented is to say that he is—for the moment—
not present. It sounds rather shocking to ears which have grown
unused to such crude anthropomorphisms to hear that God is ill
or away from home or incapacitated. Yet such language is not
so very absurd. Like Buber's phrase 'divine darkness', it accepts
the challenge set by the impossibility of experiencing God in
our age as present and immediate.

Christ represents the absent God so long as God does not
permit us to see himself. For the time being Christ takes God's
place, stands in for the God who no longer presents himself to
us directly, and who no longer brings us into his presence in the
manner claimed by earlier religious experience. Christ holds
the place of this now absent God open for him in our midst.
For without Christ, we should have to 'sack' the God who does
not show up, who has left us. We should have no reason to wait
for him, no reason not to write him off as dead. We could then
indicate our acquiescence in our replaceability and interpret

our place in the total scheme of things on the analogy of the machine and its parts. If the indivisible freedom of all men had not attained consciousness in Christ—and freedom is the New Testament equivalent of identity—then the question about identity could be dropped; this question which has in fact been posed by God's representative in such a way that it can never again be ignored. Because Christ produced a new kind of existence in the world it is impossible ever again to abandon hope. Christ's representation is the transcendental possibility of such hope.

But in view of this hope, what Nietzsche calls the 'death of God', the fact 'that the highest values are devalued',[1] is in fact only the death of God's immediacy—the death of his unmediated first form, the dissolving of a particular conception of God in the consciousness. It is therefore unnecessary for Christ to counter Nietzsche's assertion of the death of God by affirming a naive consciousness of God. If the dialogue between Christians and non-Christians is simply a tedious exchange of affirmative and negative statements, it is certainly not Christ who speaks in this way. To assert that God 'is' is no answer to the contemporary challenge, for Nietzsche does not in fact assert that God 'is not'. His madman does not announce the commonplace widsom of an atheism which imagines it has something to say objectively about the existence or non-existence of a supreme supernatural being. Unlike the multitude of the sane, Nietzsche's madman goes about saying, 'I seek God'.[2] Nietzsche is no more concerned with God, as he is 'in himself', than the Christian faith is. This God 'in himself' is dead, is no more an object directly present to the consciousness. Nietzsche is concerned with the God who lives for us and with us. His madman mourns the manifest inactivity of God, but the thought of denying God's reality does not occur to him. Yet this inactivity is taken seriously and at the same time transformed when someone who is conscious of it (but has the hope which resists this

---

[1] Nietzsche, *The Joyful Wisdom*, Bk. III, Sec. 125.
[2] *Was bedeutet Nihilismus?* ET *The Will to Power*, 1887, pp. 167ff.

consciousness) stands in for God. When the inactive God is provisionally represented, then the two experiences—of the death of God and of faith in Christ's resurrection—are present simultaneously to join battle as to what is real.

It is not true that these two experiences are mutually exclusive. They are not contradictory opposites, but statements which are patient of dialectical mediation into a new unity, into a 'theology after the death of God'. There are tolerably many who are exposed to both experiences, that of the death of God and that of the life of Christ, and who try to be loyal to both. To try to compel a choice between them—on grounds of so-called logic, traditional orthodoxy, church theology—is to do positivism's work for it and to hand over those who have this twofold experience to the self-assured smugness of people who simply *know* that there is no God and that Christ is dead; or, worse still, to those who are equally sure that God exists and that Christ is therefore alive. But Christ is not a replacement for the dead God. He is the representative of the living God, of the God who like man is irreplaceable yet representable. For God has not yet declared himself fully within the world, nor handed over his cause in such a way that he has become superfluous. Identity is still to come; otherwise Christ merely replaced the dead God of the past. In fact, Jesus of Nazareth has kept the future open for God by 'running ahead of him', and this is precisely Christ's function right down to the present—to be God's forerunner.

But this does not only happen where men speak of God and Christ, where Christ is made explicit, where he is proclaimed and worshipped. Christ's being extends much further than the consciousness of him. His kingdom is greater than his church. Because Christ dared provisionally to represent the absent God, he is present implicitly whenever a man acts or suffers in God's stead. What does it mean to act in God's stead and to represent him? It means so to assume responsibility for the irreplaceable identity of others that it remains possible for them to attain identity. To be provisional means to run ahead to men—before

God has reached them, but in order that he may reach them. This is precisely what Christ did, but not in an exclusive sense. The provisional Christ is also the implicit Christ; the greater Christ who has gone beyond the bounds of what is said of him, beyond the *praedicatio directa*. There is in the world an anonymous Christianity, ignorant that it is Christian, making no appeal to Christ's name and authority, yet serving his cause representatively and provisionally. The task of the organized Church in relation to this anonymous or 'latent' Church (Tillich) is the education of the consciousness. It must seek to further faith's comprehension of itself; give an account of itself; and reflect on, promote, and practise the presentation of the faith as a provisional representation of God.

Someone may object here that the term 'Christ' in this context becomes a mere cipher or metaphor, doing duty for something else—in fact for the 'new being' (Tillich) as irreplaceable identity.

As for the term 'cipher', this connotes no less than the older term 'message' or even the term 'gospel'. It is news to someone about something. And Christ is in fact news to the world about the real life. The question to be faced by the Christian faith today is whether this cipher can be finally broken, deciphered and so become superfluous. Clearly this would only be the case in a world which no longer needed this message, having taken note of it as information received and having acted on it. So long as this is not the case, the deciphering has not yet been fully successful. It may even be said that in an inhuman world the name 'Christ' is an unbreakable cipher, an 'absolute metaphor', which unlike the classic metaphor is not bound by the analogy between the reality and the image. So far from being an *adequatio rei* it stems not so much from a comparison as from a leap. We arrive at a conception of Christ's love not, or only in small measure, by way of analogy with our previous experiences, but rather *via negationis*. The absolute metaphor 'Christ' contains a negation of all 'godless' relationships; it contains the promise of identity within its representative provisionality.

The cipher 'Christ' is the mode in which Jesus continues alive to the end of the world—as the consciousness of those who represent God and claim him for each other. Where this representative claim on God is made, the implicit Christ is present. For it is not only Christ who represents God in the world. Christ's friends and brothers also represent God by allowing God—and this means necessarily those as well who need him—time.

21

CHRIST'S IDENTIFICATION WITH GOD

The Proclamation of God

CHRIST REPRESENTS THE absent God by allowing him time to appear. He identifies himself with the one who for the present is not the one he could be. He claims this God on our behalf. Here again representation rests, firstly, on the absence or incapacity of the one who must be represented, in this case the dead God, and secondly, on the provisionality of the representative who for the time being assumes the role of the one represented. Because God does not intervene to establish his cause, Christ appears in his place. He comforts those whom, up to now, God has left in the lurch, he heals those who do not understand God, feeds those whom God allows to go hungry.

But all this he does as one who identifies himself with the absent God. All representation begins with the representative's identification of himself with those he represents: the teacher with the pupil, the judge with the condemned, Jesus with the tax-collectors. Yet, as is clear from this last example, identification always includes non-identity, otherwise it would be no more than mere sociability, naive egalitarianism. The difference preserves the reality of the act of identification. Identification is a relation between those who are differentiated, which continues therefore during the process, a process which hardens when it attains its end in non-differentiation.

The content of the gospel can be described as follows: Christ identifies himself with God in the area of non-identity. For Christ is 'like all others', indistinguishable from them in poverty, weakness and mortality. In the words of the Christmas carol,

'God has left his heavenly throne and must journey on earth's ways'. This mythical picture, using the imagery of space and the cosmos, can be translated into the temporal terms of human history. The God whom men believed in, and for centuries worshipped as the God who sits on his heavenly throne, comes to be regarded instead, from a definite date onwards, from the time of the man Jesus of Nazareth, as a disinherited and homeless being whom one might any day meet at any street corner. Ever since Jesus claimed this once enthroned God for the everyday life of ordinary people, God has become indistinguishable. This representative identification with God, carried through by Christ provisionally and as forerunner, is the transcendental possibility of love.

Yet Christ at the same time preserved the difference between him and God. He only represents God. He does not replace him. It would be a mistake to interpret incarnation as God's complete self-emptying into human form. This would mean that we had already had all there was to have from God and nothing remained to look for from him. On the basis of this non-identity, Christ lays claim to God on our behalf, assuming responsibility for the absent God and taking up the cause of the unavailable God.

Here too the question arises how we are to interpret this in the light of the modern experience of the death of God? Jean Paul once dreamt that Christ after death called down to the souls of the departed that God was dead. The Christ, is the essay in which he describes this dream, succeeds in identifying himself with modern men, with their fears and longings, in a remarkable way—and in a way quite unthinkable for a churchified Christ. Instead of keeping his distance, instead of excluding himself on the basis of some superior certainty or some indestructible bond with God, this Christ identified himself with his brothers even to the depths of the basic experience of atheism.

And when I looked up to the immeasurable world for the Divine Eye, it glared upon me from an empty bottomless socket; and

Eternity lay brooding upon the chaos and gnawed it and ruminated it.[1]

Since our concern here is not with the history of thought, we can disregard the fact that in Jean Paul's nightmare the liberating word is not spoken by Christ but by the essayist when he wakens from his dream. It is the essayist who does what it was Christ's office to do, namely, to proclaim God for us. It is the essayist who summons the absent God and by means of his essay expels the fear that God does not exist.

If ever my heart were so unhappy and withered that all the feelings which assert the existence of God should be destroyed, I would terrify myself with my essay, and it would heal me and give me back my feelings again.[2]

This footnote to the essay, which itself remains an unrelieved atheistic nightmare, is not to be taken as a retractation of the vision, or even simply as a pious didactic afterthought. On the contrary, as an attempt to 'believe in God atheistically' it remains certainty in uncertainty, made possible by the representative who proclaims the absent God for us. Here too, identity, as an assurance that 'the Eternal loves his whole world', continues only as identity in difference, made possible by the *identificatio aliena*.

It is not for us to prophesy whether the Christian faith will once more emerge from this 'certainty in uncertainty', from this equivocation between doubt and faith, into some other form of immediate certainty. Attempts in this direction have up to now ended in pure dogmatism or various kinds of salvation positivism, making Christians more isolated from the world than ever, since solutions of this sort soon became anachronistic in a world which could, and can, only laugh in astonishment at their massive certainties. There is in fact no evidence except that provided by representative identification, and no greater certainty than that of the proclaimed God. The fact that Christ identified himself with God is the only possible ground for be-

[1] Jean Paul Friedrich Richter, *Werke*, München, 1959, Vol. XI, p. 269. ET *Flower, Fruit and Thorn Pieces*, Leipzig, 1871, Vol. I, p. 282.
[2] *Ibid.*, p. 278.

lieving in God today. This identifying claim to God is no mere assertion of an already existing reality in which the individual may participate by means of identification. The situation is not that God (a) exists and therefore (b) cares 'also for thee'. Such a pattern of proclamation would still rest on a naive theism. Nor on the other hand is this identification a metaphysical invention, producing from itself the God the world needs. This too would imply a failure to understand Christ's courage in claiming God on our behalf. Resorting to mythical language, which cannot be dispensed with altogether simply in the interests of a demythicized understanding, we may say that God himself changed when he allowed Christ to play his role under the changed conditions.

The One Who Plays God's Role

God has changed. What happened to Moses at the burning bush belongs to an irrevocable past. What St Francis felt and experienced is no longer open to us to experience as something immediate. Luther's anxieties can be explained by the psychoanalysts and stripped of their unconditionality. The progressive awakening of the consciousness has excluded these possibilities of attaining certainty about God. In whatever way we may interpret the objectifications of God in the past—miracles, providential dispositions, channels of continuing revelation—such objectifications have been carried away by the flood of advancing critical consciousness. We are no longer under any necessity to attribute these objectifications to God, to see his hand in domains ruled by historical, sociological, and psychological laws, or where blind chance pursues its course.

In this changed world, God needs actors to take his part. So long as the curtain has not rung down and the play still goes on, God's role cannot be left unfilled. God's leading player is Christ. Christ takes the part of God in the world, plays this role which without him would remain unfilled. His identification with God takes place, so to speak, behind the ontological problem of God's being (a problem clearly insoluble with the means available to our ontology), and makes that problem anachronistic, since God is present in Christ's playing of his part, though no longer as the directly experienced God.

We have to rid ourselves of the idea that the alienation of Christ, described in the hymn in *Philippians* we have already mentioned, was a brief transient stage, ending after some thirty years and superseded as quickly as possible by a return to the original situation—God in heaven, we on earth. No! In Christ God himself left the immediacy of heaven, abandoned the security of home, for ever. He mediated himself, went out from himself into unrecognizability, into non-differentiation. That this is God, who has in this way become unrecognizable, is the claim made by his player. The very God of power was played under conditions of helplessness. The very God who is the meaning of home was played under conditions of homelessness, in the far country. Christ, having left behind the life of security, claimed God for this new mode of existence—powerless, homeless, in alienation.

This way of representing the one who once existed—immediately and unrepresentably—at the same time changed the one so represented. Because God mediated himself into the world, all immediacy has come to an end since Christ. God now appears in mediation, in representation. Christ plays God's role in the world—that and nothing else is what incarnation means. With this way of mediation, there is of course no longer any room for lordship, or power, or any of the other kingly attributes of God. The Christ who represents God has come into the world in such a way that his representation is now the only possible experience of God: a religious experience, but not in the usual sense of one which culminates in a direct experience of the holy, of the *fascinans* and the *tremendum*. Of course, the new profane and worldly representation of God, established in helplessness and suffering, does not abolish the older form of religious experience, which continues tenaciously both within and outside the church. But it does make such religion superfluous—merely the survival of something man no longer needs, and which diminishes in power and influence the more man's social and natural ills are eliminated. The new and progressive reality of the represented God, who is himself absent, shows that retreat to a God, experienced as present, is simply a private affair with no claim whatever to authority.

What can be real for us is the actor who plays God's role, the leading player who is followed by many others. What he, the leading player, did—we can do too. Namely, play the role of God in conditions of helplessness. We can claim God for each other. Certainly this play-acting of ours retains the provisional character of all theatrical performances. God, too, is not so fully represented by his representative as to leave nothing of himself still to come. Nevertheless, the identification with God, which Christ ventured and pioneered, means that this identification is at the same time possible for us. We, too, can now play God for one another.

22

CHRIST'S DEPENDENCE ON GOD

CHRIST PUT HIMSELF in the place of God. For this blasphemy
he was put to death. Yet he remained at a distance from the God,
to whom he laid claim—a distance which makes no claim to
existence in identity, as of right, on the basis of the act of identification. Christ's identification with God, his claim on God,
remain non-identity. For only non-identity leaves an open
future. If Christ were identical with God, we would have nothing further to expect, except Christ. But because he only represents God, only acts in place of God, only plays God's role—
helps out the absent one, supports the helpless one—this difference keeps open the possibility that what Christ achieved here
and now is not exhaustive. By its provisionality, representation
makes hope possible. As identification, it is love in the pregnant
sense of existence for others. But because Christ remains dependent on the acceptance or rejection of the God he represents
in the world, he needs, as his representative, faith. Christ remains dependent on the acceptance or rejection of the one he
represents. He acts 'in the name of God', not in his own name.
He puts himself unreservedly into the hands of the God who
can accept or reject him. It can of course be said that by the
resurrection God has already indicated His final acceptance of
Christ's cause. But of what use is this past resurrection if it does
not also happen today; if it is merely an isolated fact without
any continuation; if, in other words, it produces no change in
the world? What would be the point of talking of the resurrection if God did not identify himself with Christ's cause, today
and tomorrow and the next day? Christ himself, at all events,

was not assured that his identification with God was identity. He remained dependent. And whenever we do the same as Christ did, namely lay claim to God for each other, we too make ourselves dependent on God, by putting our existence at risk.

Christ maintains the independence of God, the price paid being his own dependence. He plays God's role, but it is a role. The two elements—identity with the God he plays, and difference from the God who does not appear here but remains invisible—are present at all times. Christ acts *as if* he were God. He dictates to death, issues commands to the forces of nature, determines men's destiny; at times as if he alone were lord of the world. And in doing so he effects the dissolution of the ancient world and its religion, as his condemnation shows. An ordinary man claims to be lord of the sabbath, master of the law; and with that the reserved space, hitherto left free for God, becomes ordinary and profane, belonging now to society. Yet Christ only 'plays' this role; he is still at the mercy of what we do to him. He depends upon God by depending on us and living by our decisions. But that is to say that God depends on us, that he is at risk because he has linked his destiny with ours. In traditional theology, on the basis of the hymn in Phillipians, this self-surrender of God is known as *kenosis*: God empties himself. By representing God, Christ made himself defenceless, entering anonymously into the world of men. He who had the form of a slave, experienced humiliations and (what had hitherto been alien to him and to God) suffering. He voluntarily shouldered man's destiny as self-estrangement and life in non-identity. In mythical terms, he left behind the heaven where he had ruled with God in glory, keeping back for himself no trace of this glory—not even a modicum, a 'thief's loot', of something supremely precious—but abandoned all immediacy to God in the interests of complete dependence on the God who mediates himself.

But how are we, in post-metaphysical, post-theistic terms, to interpret this radical dependence accepted by Christ? How could we possibly, in this matter, 'have the same mind in us as was in Christ Jesus'? What heaven do *we* have to leave behind? What does the end of immediacy mean for the individual? Can the 'new being' be conceived at all without some immediate proximity to God, some direct experience of Him?

It is clear that the Christian myth presupposes a universe which is multi-storied, a picture which has not been left behind simply by discarding as old fashioned the idea of a localized heaven and the notion of a temporal pre-existence of the Son of God, without discovering any modern equivalent. Heaven or being with God is a naive, mythical form of what we call in secular language the longing for happiness. This elemental longing for happiness is just as much part of the modern human condition as the equally incontrovertible hope of a *beyond* probably was for that of men in earlier periods. We regard this longing for happiness as the horizon of a world view—a horizon which we cannot discard at will, any more than the man of late antiquity or of the late middle ages could discard at will his vision of the soul's salvation after death. If we take seriously this inner-worldly horizon of the longing for happiness—instead of viewing it with suspicion as moralists—we can see that it fulfils the same function as this earlier 'vision' and is no less 'Christian'. Both the reference to a *beyond* and the longing for happiness are indirectly related to salvation. Both are equally distant from it, yet both expect and think of it as something immediate.

No one can reorientate others, not even himself, from happiness to 'salvation'. And no more could Christ reorientate men from their 'reward' (which surely from very early on must have been also interpreted in terms of post-mortal bliss) to a spiritualized salvation. On the contrary, salvation appeared at that time in the religious context of the expectation of a world *beyond*. Just as today it is only in the religious context of the expectation for *this* world that this genuinely mythical longing for happiness appears. But in both cases the religious context is relativized and shattered by Christ. The world beyond *and* this world; flight from the world *and* flight into the world; the immediacy of heaven *and* the immediacy of the earth—all stand in the shadow of the greater reality, the shadow of the cross which abolishes them all.

Christ did not cling to his being with God like a thief clutching his loot—but we cling longingly to happiness as something supremely precious. If Christ had been as we are, he would never have left heaven. But he left heaven and let happiness go. And this was the end of the old immediacy to God, and the beginning of the 'new being'. In fact there is only one chance for man to cut loose from his so deep-rooted longing for happiness; the way of love. In the existence for others, the search for personal identity becomes unnecessary. Love does not insist on heaven. It does not need it. Not that love itself is heaven, still less that it renounces it! But love 'represents' the absent God in the world. It 'counts' on the heaven which appears here. It does not anxiously clutch hold of God, like so much loot, and it is no longer anxious for the immediate. For along the way of mediation, the way of alienation into existence for others (which always means existence in the far country, in pain, and in renunciation of one's own possibilities), what has been given away reappears again, just as the reward appears in the teaching of Jesus only when it has ceased to be the calculated aim of action.[1] Happiness, our most fragile possession, thrives only when it is not anxiously sought after. For identity is not, as it might first appear, the most immediate of things, but something indirect and mediated. That is why, in Christian thought, it can only appear as representation, in which the representative makes himself dependent upon the represented.

Christ's dependence, his self-surrender, is the cause of his suffering. Christ only represents the God of life, he does not replace him. Because he remains dependent on God, he suffers and bears the pains of God in the world. Every form of substitute for life fills in the gaps in life and whitewashes a defective existence. The dependent representative, on the contrary, keeps

[1] Luke 6.35; Matt. 6.3f.

open the gap which represents God's life; and a gap left open means, concretely, a wound which cannot be closed and healed so long as God's identity has not been attested in the world.

The dependence on another's verdict which representation involves, explains the capacity to suffer. If Christ had not been dependent—if he had been a king, a hero, a victor, rather than a precursor, an advocate, a player—he would not have been the peerless man of sorrows who by suffering keeps open God's place in the world. The love of which the Gospel speaks is simply the radical intervention of one irreplaceable being for another; an identification which is provisional and which makes its agent dependent. Christ identified himself with God and thereby made himself dependent on God's attaining identity himself. Anyone who identifies himself with Christ likewise represents God in the world, in suffering and in transitoriness.

Is it then a question of God's identity in the world? Yes—at least for those who cannot renounce man's identity and their own irreplaceability. They will go on expecting God to become identical with himself. Certainly his identity is not plainer and more visible than that of his irreplaceable friends. His identity, too, appears ambiguous and veiled, hidden in the adventure of the world's emergence.

But what is hidden is not forgotten. Nor is God's identity so completely emptied into the world that it too could be replaced by something else. If there is any justification for speaking of God's 'worldliness', it cannot be in the sense that He is dissolved into the world; if only because the present condition of the world is not so 'God-tinted' as, on such an assumption, it would need to be. God is not immanent in our history, because his identity in this history remains still future. Jesus continues to hang on the cross and will not let himself be persuaded to come down from the cross by those who would prefer him to do so, whether to ascend into heaven or to be buried, once and for all. We still cannot expect an end to humiliation and depersonalization. In a world whose characteristic is the interchangeability of all men, God's identity is still in the future. For Christ to come down from the cross would mean his consent to the depersonalization of men. By continuing to suffer, he maintains his kingdom which has not yet appeared, he remains a powerless advocate in man's behalf, the actor who plays the role of God.

For God is not just proclaimed, not just announced and promised by prophets; he is also represented in the world. Only in this way does his kingdom remain open and escape oblivion. Christ lives and is present wherever God is represented. In representation, God's kingdom is attested, but as one which has not been built here. The reminder Christ gives us of identity is the consciousness of the kingdom which has not yet appeared, a consciousness kept awake in the form of pain. Representation permits a form of suffering which does not make us blind, impotent, and sterile, which does not succumb to the self-destruction which the sufferers bring upon themselves and the world. 'Man is challenged to participate in the sufferings of God at the hands of a godless world.'[1] The man who participates in 'the sufferings of God' will go on waiting for God's identity, or, as it was called in the older terminology, the kingdom of God.

Even where men imagine they can dispense with this identity of God, the representative answers for God and holds his place open for him. Christ guarantees the unforgotten kingdom, and enables us to live in postponement. Here he remains unsurpassed—there is no place nearer God than that which he occupies provisionally, the place of the protagonist and placeminder, of the advocate and actor. Christ is only surpassed by the new heaven and the new earth for which we long. Surpassed by nothing else except this, as only he himself would wish.

Even after his death as One who confronts us directly, God still has a future in Christ. Since God did not cancel his promise, Christ did not regard it as his task to go on repeating this promise. What he did was to represent the kingdom of identity

---

[1] Dietrich Bonhoeffer, *Letters and Papers from Prison*, SCM Press, London, 1953, p. 166; Fontana Books, 1959, p. 122.

which has not yet appeared. This kingdom has 'drawn near' in this representative who keeps open God's place in the world, who, by doing so, allows God time and a future. God suffers by reason of his unrealized, or only partly realized, existence in the world. He suffers by reason of his defeats; which no one knows better than his players in the world, who play this part in conditions of helplessness. God wills to be represented. He has made himself representable. He has made himself conditional, provisional. He has become dependent; he has mediated himself into the world. He became man.

CONCLUSION

The Helplessness of God in the World

CHRIST TOOK OVER God's role in the world, but in the process it was changed into the role of the helpless God. The absent God whom Christ represents is the God who is helpless in this world. Experience of this helpless God was not altogether unfamiliar to earlier centuries, in spite of the immediacy assumed in theism and the omnipotence which goes with it. Yet it was only after the death of God that this experience of the helpless God became the decisive factor. In his last letters, Dietrich Bonhoeffer spoke often of this helplessness of God in the world. Indeed, this experience of God's helplessness may be regarded as the basis of Bonhoeffer's non-religious interpretation of Christian concepts.

God allows himself to be edged out of the world and on to the cross. God is weak and powerless in the world, and that is exactly the way, the only way, in which he can be with us and help us. This is the decisive difference between Christianity and all religions. Man's religiosity makes him look in his distress to the power of God in the world; he uses God as a *Deus ex machina*. The Bible however directs him to the powerlessness and suffering of God; only a suffering God can help.[1]

In this sense, the atheism based on the 'rock of suffering'[2]—that is to say, an atheism rooted in the insoluble problem of evil—is still a religion in Bonhoeffer's sense. For the God who is arraigned because of the suffering of the innocent is really the omnipotent God, the king, father, and ruler, who is above the world. Modern man rightly indicts this God. And none of the theological devices used to silence this indictment can

---

[1] Bonhoeffer, *Letters and Papers*, p. 164; p. 122 (Fontana).
[2] Georg Büchner, poet, 1813-1837.

suppress the truth of this questioning of the almighty God. Certainly no dogmatic positing of a God who reduces us to silence because he alone has the right to speak.

If we refuse to drop this question, and do not piously suppress it, we are led to abandon the theistic God. The open-eyed, deliberate atheism of modern times has not drawn its strength from the wells of scientific rationalism and historical criticism. Its existential argument (in Büchner, Heine, Crabbe, and Jacobsen) has been the pain, injustice and suffering endured by the innocent. In all religions, a question mark has been set against the omnipotent and serene gods by the sufferings of men. But only in Christ does the concept of a suffering God appear. Here alone is it the suffering of God which is shouldered by a man. Only in Christ does it become clear that we can put God to death because he has put himself in our hands. Only since Christ has God become dependent on us. Christ did not identify himself with a calm spectator of all our troubles. Christ, by his teaching, life and death, made plain the helplessness of God in the world; the suffering of unrequited and unsuccessful love. 'Jesus does not call men to a new religion'—one in which God would be directly accessible to us—'but to life' in the presence of the absent and inactive God.[1] Bonhoeffer goes on to ask: 'What is the nature of that life, that participation in the powerlessness of God in the world?' The answer, surely, is the representation of God on earth.

If, for the nineteenth century, suffering was still the 'rock of atheism', nothing is so eloquent of God in our own century as his defeat in the world. That God in the world has been, and still is, mocked and tortured, burnt and gassed: that is the rock of the Christian faith which rests all its hope on God attaining his identity. This pain is inextinguishable; this hope can never be taken away. What Christians share in common is 'their participation in the sufferings of God in Christ. That is their faith.'[2] In this faith they know that God is helpless and needs

---

[1] *Op. cit.*, p. 167; p. 123 (Fontana).
[2] *Op. cit.*, p. 167; p. 123 (Fontana).

help. When the time was fulfilled, God had done something for us for long enough. He put himself at risk, made himself dependent upon us, identified himself with the non-identical. From now on, it is high time for us to do something for him.

READING LIST

BLOCH, Ernst *Das Prinzip Hoffnung*, Aufbau Verlag, Berlin, 1954-59 Frankfurt, 1959.

BONHOEFFER, Dietrich *Ethics*, ed. Eberhard Bethge, tr. Neville Horton Smith (SCM Press, London, 1955), Fontana Library, Collins, London, 1964.
Letters and Papers from Prison, Fontana Books, Collins, London, 1959 (originally SCM Press, London, 1953). Revised and illustrated translation, SCM Press, London, 1967.

BUBER, Martin *Tales of the Hasidim*, tr. Olga Marx, Thames and Hudson, London, 1956 (2 vols.).
Two Types of Faith, tr. Norman P. Goldhawk, Routledge and Kegan Paul, London, 1951.

BUHR, Heinrich *Der Glaube—was ist das?* Pfullingen, 1963.

BULTMANN, Rudolf *Glauben und Verstehen*, Vol. 1 Mohr, Tübingen, 1933.
Jesus and the Word, tr. L. P. Smith & E. H. Lantero, Scribner, New York, 1958, Fontana Library, Collins, London.

CAMUS, Albert *The Rebel*, tr. Anthony Bower, Hamish Hamilton, London, 1953.

EBELING, Gerhard *The Nature of Faith*, tr. Ronald Gregor Smith, Collins, London, 1961; Muhlenberg Press, Philadelphia, 1962.

GEHLEN, Arnold *Die Seele im technischen Zeitalter, Sozialpsychologische Probleme in der industriellen Gesellschaft*, Rowohlt, Hamburg, 1957.

GOGARTEN, Friedrich *Verhängnis und Hoffnung der Neuzeit, Die Säkularsierung als theologisches Problem*, Friedrich Vorwerk Verlag, Stuttgart, ²1958.
Die Verkündigung Jesu Christi, Verlag Lambert Schneider, Heidelberg, 1948.
Was ist Christentum? Vandenhoeck & Ruprecht, Göttingen, 1956.

HEIDEGGER, Martin *Being and Time*, tr. J. Macquarrie & E. Robinson, SCM Press, London, 1962.

HIRSCH, Emanuel *Die idealistische Philosophie und das Christentum*, Gütersloh, 1926.

JONAS, Hans *Gnosis und spätantiker Geist*, Vol. I Göttingen, [2]1954, ET, *The Gnostic Religion, The Message of the Alien God, and the Beginnings of Christianity*. Beacon Press, Boston, 1958.
Zwischen Nichts und Ewigkeit, Zur Lehre vom Menschen. Göttingen, 1963.

LOEGSTRUP, Knud E. C. *Die ethische Forderung*, tr. from Danish by Rosemarie Logstrup, H. Laupp, Tübingen, 1959.

PANNENBERG, Wolfhart *Was ist der Mensch?* Göttingen, 1962.

ROBINSON, John A. T. *Honest to God*, SCM Press, London, 1963.

SCHOLEM, Gershom *Judaica*, Frankfurt, 1963.

TILLICH, Paul *The New Being*, SCM Press, London, 1956.
Auf der Grenze 1964, ET *On the Boundary*, Scribner, New York, 1966.
The Courage to Be, Yale University Press, New Haven, 1959.

WEIL, Simone *Waiting on God*, Fontana Library, Collins, London, 1959.